SEASONAL HAND KNITTED DESIGNS FOR 18" DOLLS

By Debonair Designs

Spring/Summer Collection ~ 13 patterns designed to fit American Girl Dolls®, 18" Gotz Dolls®, sized to fit 18" Dolls that share the same body type

Text and knitwear designs
Copyright © 2011 - 2013 Debonair Designs

All rights reserved.

Debonair Designs is the exclusive copyright holder in this publication and the designs and photographs contained herein. As such the copyright of this pattern book publication, it's text, photos copyright 2011 - 2013 Debonair Designs.
No part of this book may be reproduced, stored in a retrieval system, or transmitted in any form or by any means electronic, electrostatic, magnetic tape, mechanical, photocopying or otherwise without prior written permission from the copyright owner.

ISBN-10: 1490331964

ISBN-13: 978-1490331966

Author/Editor: Deborah Patterson
Styling and Designs: © 2011 - 2013 Debonair Designs
Photography: Deborah Patterson, Tekay International™
Photo Editor: Mariah Patterson
Graphic Artist: Mariah Patterson
Test Knitters: D. Rodgers, Vall Anderson
Model Dolls: Elisabeth, Jessica, Julia, Katie, Tess & Teyla

The knitwear designs in this book are copyrighted and must not be knitted for re-sale. Reproduction of this publication is protected by copyright and is sold on the condition that it be used for non commercial purposes.

Disclaimer: Debonair Designs is not affiliated with any doll or doll clothing companies.

18" DOLLS ~ SPRING/SUMMER COLLECTION

DEDICATION

For all Crafters and Knitters

*She hopes that you will understand,
the beauty of things made by hand,*

*That you will feel the mystic spell,
that every craftsman knows so well.*

*By potter's kiln, or loom,
in shed, or attic, or spare room,*

*She adds a certain magic touch,
creating things she loves so much.*

*Not simply made of wool or stone,
not for financial gain alone,*

*But made with patience, love and care,
that others may her pleasures share.*

*She does not measure time by days,
she labors long whilst others lay.*

*From misty dawn to setting sun,
until she feels her work's well done.*

*So when you buy the craftsman's wares,
you're buying from someone who cares.*

*She'll sell you treasures that never fade,
for everything has been 'Hand Made'.*

~ author unknown

SEASONAL HAND KNITTED DESIGNS FOR 18" DOLLS ~ SPRING/SUMMER COLLECTION

PHOTO INDEX

Bria Collection & Of The Earth Collection

Neapolitan Chic Collection

From The Sea Collection

by Debonair Designs ~ copyright © 2011 - 2013 Debonair Designs

CONTENTS

	Introduction	vii
	Standard Abbreviations	viii
1	**Bria Collection:**	Pg 11

Bria ~ a shawl collared sweater or cardigan
Newsboy Cap ~ a trendy flat cap
Irish Warmer ~ a ribbed stitched fishermen's sweater

2	**Of the Earth Collection:**	Pg 35

Ayanna ~ a faux fair isle stitched sweater dress
Pippi II ~ faux fair isle stitched leg warmers

3	**Neapolitan Chic Collection:**	Pg 49

Cabana ~ a chevron stitched tunic and petticoat skirt
Kimana ~ a flattering bolero jacket
Belle ~ a cloche style hat
BoHoh ~ a ribbed stitched tote bag

4	**From the Sea Collection:**	Pg 69

Adrift ~ a chevron stitched cardigan
Kiah ~ a lace stitched jump suit with bib top option
Charter ~ a ribbed stitched hooded jacket with sleeveless option
Eyelet Beret ~ a stylish eyelet beret

Meet the Models	Pg 93
About the Model Dolls	Pg 94
Acknowledgments	Pg 98
About the Author/Designer	Pg 99

SEASONAL HAND KNITTED DESIGNS FOR 18" DOLLS ~ SPRING/SUMMER COLLECTION

Charter ~ from the Sea Collection pg 84 (cover) Models: Elisabeth & Jessica

by Debonair Designs ~ copyright © 2011 - 2013 Debonair Designs

INTRODUCTION

SEASONAL HAND KNITTED DESIGNS FOR 18" DOLLS

Spring/Summer Collection

13 hand knitted pattern designs in a four collection volume that is suitable for both the beginner and seasoned knitter, created not only for your doll's seasonal wardrobe, but for you, the knitter, in celebration in the art of knitting, and in honor of my Mom, Brenda, who taught me the art of knitting at a young age.

This Spring/Summer Collection has been fashioned to coordinate with each other for complete ensembles, from the traditional options offered in the Bria Collection, to the spring cherry blossom inspired set found in the Earth Collection, along with the versatile styles of the Neapolitan Chic Collection, finishing with trendy nautical essentials from the Sea Collection, *(Charter on cover)*, each design is worked with your doll's ease of dressing in mind.

~ Debonair Designs

SEASONAL HAND KNITTED DESIGNS FOR 18" DOLLS
by Debonair Designs

Designed to fit: American Girl Dolls ®
& the comparable 18" Gotz ® Dolls,
sized for 18" dolls that share the same body type.

STANDARD ABBREVIATIONS:

K = knit

P = purl

St(s) = stitch(es)

rep = repeat

YO = yarn over (yarn over needle)

YRN = yarn round needle

Cont = continue

* = repeat instructions as directed

** = repeat instructions following the asterisks as directed

( ) = work instruction within parentheses in the place directed

[ ] = work instructions within brackets as many times as directed

sl = slip stitch

PSSO = pass slipped stitch over

K2tog = knit 2 stitches together

P2tog = purl 2 stitches together

Kfb = knit into front and back of stitch

Tbl = through back of loop

GLOSSARY:

Cast on = bind on

Cast off = bind off

Stockinette Stitch = stocking stitch

Work even = continue what you have been doing without any increases or decreases

BASIC INFORMATION:

The quantities of yarn are based on average requirements and are therefore approximate. Gauge is an average suggestion; achieved from several test knitters using stated needles and yarn recommendations, worked to the gauge given. If you have too many stitches, your tension is tight and you should change to a larger needle. If there are too few stitches, your tension is loose and you should change to a smaller needle

MATERIALS USED:

4 MEDIUM Worsted/Aran 10ply yarn similar to or like Red Heart Soft Solids ™, Caron Simply Soft ™, Patons Classic Worsted ™

Yarn Equivalent: 8 ply, Aran (UK)

SKILL LEVELS:

BEGINNER Projects for first time knitters using basic knit and purl stitches, minimal shaping

EASY Projects using basic stitches, repetitive stitch patterns, simple color changes, and simple shaping and finishing.

INTERMEDIATE Projects with a variety of stitches, such as basic cables and lace, mid level shaping and finishing.

Source: Yarn Standards.™

Bria

Bria Collection ~ Abbreviations & Tips

Standard Abbreviations:

Refer to pg viii

Special Abbreviations:

Bria Sweater/Cardigan

C2L = cross 2 left, (no cable needle) with right needle behind the first stitch on left needle, knit the second stitch through the front strand (loop), knit first stitch in usual way, allowing both to slip off

Stitch Patterns:

Moss Stitch = knit 1, purl 1 across first row, purl over the knit, knit over the purl on following row

Garter Stitch = knit every row

Stockinette Stitch = knit a row, purl a row

Tip for Sleeves: Cast on stitches for each sleeve on the same needle, using separate skeins for each sleeve, and working them at the same time

Tip for Sleeve Top Shaping: When working the cast off stitches over several rows as indicated, slip the first of the cast off stitches, then proceed with cast off, this makes for a smoother transition

Pattern Note: Worked flat: Back and forth in rows

Construction: Refer to individual pattern pages for details

Skill Level: Refer to individual pattern pages for details

Materials: Refer to individual pattern pages for quantities

4 MEDIUM Worsted/10ply yarn used for main color along
Yarn Equivalent: 8 ply, Aran (UK)

SEASONAL HAND KNITTED DESIGNS FOR 18" DOLLS ~ SPRING/SUMMER COLLECTION

BRIA COLLECTION

Models wearing **Bria** paired with **Newsboy Cap**

The Bria Collection Patterns:

Bria ~ a shawl collared sweater .... Pg 12

and cardigan .... Pg 19

Newsboy Cap ~ a trendy flat cap with peak

.... Pg 25

Irish Warmer ~ a ribbed stitched sweater

.... Pg 27

~ 2 ~

Bria Collection

Inspired by the popular and traditional shawl collars found in Irish fashion, the first set has been designed to achieve two looks each featuring the flattering neckline in both the sweater and double-breasted cardigan. The third sweater pattern follows a more classic ribbed stitched pattern throughout, paired with a trendy flat cap added for a complete look. ~ Debonair Designs

Model wearing **Irish Warmer** paired with **Newsboy Cap**

- 11 -

by Debonair Designs ~ copyright © 2011 - 2013 Debonair Designs

Bria Sweater ~ The Bria Collection

*Model wearing **Bria** paired with **Newsboy Cap***

Pattern Features: The pattern has been written out with line-by-line instructions given, including back buttonhole placement. Accenting the front is an easy to achieve cross stitch pattern using no cable needle that is flanked with traditional moss stitch, set in long sleeves and a flattering shawl collar neckline

Construction: Worked flat: Back and forth in rows, from bottom up in one piece to armholes, then each section is worked individually

Materials: 210 – 230 yards (4 - 4 ¾ ounces) of worsted weight yarn

Knitting Needles: Pair each of 3.25mm (US 3-UK/CANADIAN 10) and 3.75mm (US 5-UK/CANADIAN 9)

Notions: 5 Buttons size ½" (12mm), Darning Needle

Gauge: Using 3.75mm needles: 6 sts and 7 rows in 1in over moss stitch

Skill Level: EASY   INTERMEDIATE

Main Body: (Includes button bands worked in moss stitch at each end)

Pattern Note: smaller needles are used for shawl collar of sweater

Using larger sized needles, begin at lower edge, **cast on 78 sts,** work as follows:

Set Up Row: (K1, P1) seven times, (P2, K4) three times, P2, K10, P2, (K4, P2) three times, (P1, K1) seven times

Continue on to Stitch Pattern

by Debonair Designs ~ copyright © 2011 - 2013 Debonair Designs

Sweater ~ Bria Collection Cont

Stitch Pattern:

Row 1: (wrong side) (K1, P1) seven times, (K2, P4) three times, K2, (K1, P1) five times, K2, (P4, K2) three times, (P1, K1) seven times

Row 2: (K1, P1) seven times, (P2, C2L, K2) three times, P2, (P1, K1) five times, P2, (C2L, K2, P2) three times, (P1, K1) seven times

Row 3: as row 1

Row 4: (K1, P1) seven times, (P2, K1, C2L, K1) three times, P2, (P1, K1) five times, P2, (K1, C2L, K1, P2) three times, (P1, K1) seven times

Row 5: as row 1

Row 6: (K1, P1) seven times, (P2, K2, C2L) three times, P2, (P1, K1) five times, P2, (K2, C2L, P2) three times, (P1, K1) seven times

Row 7: as row 1

These seven rows form the pattern stitch

Continue as follows:

Row 8: (1st buttonhole) (K1, P1) seven times, (P2, C2L, K2) three times, P2, (P1, K1) five times, P2, (C2L, K2, P2) three times, (P1, K1) five times, P1, K1, YO, K2tog

Rows 9 – 13: Repeat rows 3 – 7, once more

Rows 14 – 19: Repeat rows 2 – 7, once more

Row 20: (2nd buttonhole) (K1, P1) seven times, (P2, C2L, K2) three times, P2, (P1, K1) five times, P2, (C2L, K2, P2) three times, (P1, K1) five times, P1, K1, YO, K2tog

Rows 21 – 25: Repeat rows 3 – 7, once more

Continue to Divide

Divide:

Next Row: (K1, P1) seven times, P2, cast off 8 sts, K1, P2, C2L, K2, P2, (P1, K1) five times, P2, C2L, K2, P2, K2, cast off 8sts, P1, (P1, K1) seven times

Continue on to Right Back

Sweater ~ Bria Collection

Right Back: (Includes button band worked in moss stitch)

Wrong side facing, work on **first 16 sts** in Right Back Stitch Pattern

Right Back Stitch Pattern:

Row 1: * K1, P1, rep from * to last 2 sts; K2

Row 2: P2, * P1, K1, rep from * to end

These two rows form the pattern stitch

Continue as follows:

Rows 3 – 4: Repeat rows 1 – 2, **one more time**

Row 5: as row 1

Row 6: (3rd buttonhole) P2, * P1, K1, rep from * to last 2 sts; YO, K2tog

Rows 7 – 16: Repeat rows 1 – 2, **five more times**

Row 17: as row 1

Row 18: (4th buttonhole) as row 6

Rows 19 – 23: Repeat rows 1 – 2, **two more times**, then work **row 1** *only*, **once more**

Continue on to Shape Shoulder

Shape Shoulder:

Next Row: Cast off 8sts, * K1, P1, rep from * to last st; K1

Cast off remaining 8 sts

Continue on to Front

Front:

Wrong side facing, rejoin yarn to **center 30 sts**, work as follows:

Next Row: P2, K2, P4, K2, (K1, P1) five times, K2, P4, K2, P2

* Pattern Note: This next row divides the section in readiness for neck shaping

Next Row: K2, P2, K1, C2L, K1, P2, cast off center 10 sts in pattern, P1, K1, C2L, K1, P2, K2

Continue on to Neck Shaping Right Side

Sweater ~ Bria Collection Cont

Neck Shaping Right Side: Wrong side facing, work as follows:

Row 1: P2, K2, P4, K2

Row 2: P2, K2, C2L, P2, K2

Row 3: as row 1

Row 4: P2tog, C2L, K2, P2, K2

Row 5: P2, K2, P4, K1

Row 6: P1, K1, C2L, K1, P2, K2

Row 7: as row 5

Row 8: K2tog, K1, C2L, P2, K2 = *8sts*

Continue and work <u>even</u> as follows:

Row 9: P2, K2, P4

Row 10: C2L, K2, P2, K2

Row 11: as row 9

Row 12: K1, C2L, K1, P2, K2

Row 13: as row 9

Row 14: K2, C2L, P2, K2

Rows 15 – 16: Repeat rows 9 – 10, <u>once more</u>

Row 17: as row 9

Row 18: as row 12

Row 19: as row 9

Row 20: as row 14

Row 21: as row 9

Row 22: K4, P2, K2

Row 23: as row 9

Cast off all sts, cont as follows:

Neck Shaping Left Side: Wrong side facing, rejoin yarn to left side stitches, work as follows:

Row 1: K2, P4, K2, P2

Row 2: K2, P2, K2, C2L, P2

Row 3: as row 1

Row 4: K2, P2, C2L, K2, P2tog

Row 5: K1, P4, K2, P2

Row 6: K2, P2, K1, C2L, K1, P1

Row 7: as row 5

Row 8: K2, P2, K3, K2tog = *8sts*

Continue and work <u>even</u> as follows:

Row 9: P4, K2, P2

Row 10: K2, P2, C2L, K2

Row 11: as row 9

Row 12: K2, P2, K1, C2L, K1

Row 13: as row 9

Row 14: K2, P2, K2, C2L

Rows 15 – 16: Repeat rows 9 – 10, <u>once more</u>

Row 17: as row 9

Row 18: as row 12

Row 19: as row 9

Row 20: as row 14

Row 21: as row 9

Row 22: K2, P2, K4

Row 23: as row 9

Cast off all stitches, cont on to **Left Back**

Sweater ~ Bria Collection

Left Back: (Includes button band worked in moss stitch)

Wrong side facing, rejoin yarn to **remaining 16 sts**, work in Left Back Stitch Pattern

Left Back Stitch Pattern:

Row 1: K2, * P1, K1, rep from * to end

Row 2: * K1, P1, rep from * to last 2 sts; P2

These two rows form the pattern stitch

Continue as follows:

Rows 3 – 22: Repeat rows 1 – 2, **ten more times**

Continue on to Shape Shoulder

Shape Shoulder:

Next Row: Cast off 8sts, * K1, P1, rep from * to last st; K1

Cast off remaining 8 sts

Right sides together, join shoulders

Continue on to Shawl Collar

Shawl Collar:

Pattern Note: Using smaller needles throughout, the shawl collar is worked in two pieces; this allows the back to be open for the back button closure

Left Side: Right side facing, begin at button band edge of left back, pick up and knit 10 sts across back and shoulder seam, 19 sts down left front ending at beginning of center cast off stitches *= 29 sts*

Continue and work in Shawl Collar Stitch Pattern

Shawl Collar Stitch Pattern:

Row 1: K1, * P1, K1, rep from * to end

Row 2: * K1, P1, rep from * to last st; K1

These two rows form the **moss stitch** pattern

Continue as follows:

Rows 3 – 12: Repeat rows 1 – 2, **five more times**

Cast off loosely in pattern, continue on to Right Side

Right Side: Right side facing, begin at end of front center cast off stitches, pick up and knit 19 sts along right front, 10 sts across shoulder seam and right back *= 29 sts*

Row 1: K1, * P1, K1, rep from * to end

Row 2: (top 5th buttonhole) * K1, P1, rep from * to last 3 sts; K1, YO, K2tog

These two rows form the **moss stitch** pattern

Continue as follows:

Rows 3 – 12: Repeat rows 1 – 2, **five more times,** omit buttonhole, work moss stitch pattern as established

Cast off loosely in pattern

Continue on to Complete Collar

Complete Collar: Sew down left side of collar to center cast off stitches at front, overlap right side of collar and sew down at front.

Continue on to Sleeves

Sweater/Cardigan ~ Bria Collection

Sleeves: Both alike

Pattern Note: The sleeves are the same for both the sweater and cardigan
Sleeve Tip: refer to pg 10

Using larger sized needles throughout, begin at cuff edge, **cast on 28 sts,** work in Cuff Stitch Pattern

Cuff Stitch Pattern:

Row 1: P2,(K4, P2) four times, K1, P1

Row 2: P1, K1,(K2, P4) four times, K2

Row 3: P2 (C2L, K2, P2) four times, K1, P1

Row 4: as row 2

Row 5: P2, (K1, C2L, K1, P2) four times, K1, P1

Row 6: as row 2

Row 7: P2, (K2, C2L, P2) four times, K1, P1

Row 8: as row 2

These eight rows **complete** the cuff

Continue on to Sleeve Stitch Pattern

Sleeve Stitch Pattern:

Row 1: * K1, P1, rep from * to end

Row 2: * P1, K1, rep from * to end

These two rows form the **moss stitch** pattern

Continue as follows:

Rows 3 – 30: Repeat rows 1 – 2, **fourteen more times**

Continue on to Shape Sleeve Top

Shaping Tip: refer to pg 10

Shape Sleeve Top:

Right side facing, work as follows:

Row 1: Cast off 3 sts, * K1, P1, rep from * to end

Row 2: Cast off 3 sts, * P1, K1, rep from * to last st; P1

Row 3: Cast off 3 sts, P1, * K1, P1, rep from * to last st; K1

Row 4: Cast off 3 sts, * K1, P1, rep from * to last st; K1

Row 5: as row 1

Row 6: Cast off 3 sts, * P2tog; rep from * to last st; P1 = *6 sts*

Cast off remaining sts, continue on to Complete

Sweater/Cardigan ~ Bria Collection

Complete: Right sides together, join sleeve seams to beginning of sleeve top shaping. Wrong side facing, insert to cast off stitches of armhole opening, sew evenly around opening. Sew on buttons.

Completed Sweater Measurement: approx. 6 ½" from cast on edge to shoulder seam, with a sleeve length of approx. 6" from cuff edge to top of sleeve cap.

Bria Cardigan ~ Bria Collection

Pattern Features: The pattern has been written out with line-by-line instructions given, including buttonhole placement. Set in long sleeves and a flattering shawl collar neckline

Construction: Worked flat: Back and forth in rows, from bottom up in one piece to armholes, then each section is worked individually

Materials: 210 – 230 yards (4 - 4 ¾ ounces) of worsted weight yarn

Knitting Needles: Pair of 3.75mm throughout (US 5-UK/CANADIAN 9)

Notions: 6 Buttons size ½" (12mm), Darning Needle

Gauge: Using 3.75mm needles: 6 sts and 7 rows in 1in over moss stitch

Skill Level: EASY   INTERMEDIATE

Models wearing **Bria** paired with **Newsboy Cap**

Main Body: (Includes button bands worked in moss stitch at each end)

Begin at lower edge, **cast on 78 sts,** work as follows:

Set Up Row: (K1, P1) seven times, (P2, K4) three times, P2, K10, P2, (K4, P2) three times, (P1, K1) seven times

Continue on to **Stitch Pattern**

Cardigan ~ Bria Collection Cont

Stitch Pattern:

Row 1: (wrong side) (K1, P1) five times, (K2, P4) three times, K2, (K1, P1) nine times, (K2, P4) three times, K2, (K1, P1) five times

Row 2: (P1, K1) five times, P2, (C2L, K2, P2) three times, (P1, K1) nine times, P2, (C2L, K2, P2) three times, (P1, K1) five times

Row 3: as row 1

Row 4: (P1, K1) five times, P2, (K1, C2L, K1, P2) three times, (P1, K1) nine times, P2, (K1, C2L, K1, P2) three times, (P1, K1) five times

Row 5: as row 1

Row 6: (P1, K1) five times, P2, (K2, C2L, P2) three times, (P1, K1) nine times, P2, (K2, C2L, P2) three times, (P1, K1) five times

Row 7: as row 1

These seven rows form the pattern stitch

Continue as follows:

Row 8: (1st buttonholes) P1, K1, YO, K2tog, (P1, K1) two times, YO, K2tog, P2, (C2L, K2, P2) three times, (P1, K1) nine times, P2, (C2L, K2, P2) three times, (P1, K1) five times

Rows 9 – 13: Repeat rows 3 – 7, **once more**

Rows 14 – 19: Repeat rows 2 – 7, **once more**

Row 20: (2nd buttonholes) P1, K1, YO, K2tog, (P1, K1) two times, YO, K2tog, P2, (C2L, K2, P2) three times, (P1, K1) nine times, P2, (C2L, K2, P2) three times, (P1, K1) five times

Rows 21 – 25: Repeat rows 3 – 7, **once more**

Continue to Divide

Divide:

Next Row: (P1, K1) five times, P2, C2L, K2, P2, cast off 8 sts, K1, P2, (P1, K1) nine times, P2, K2, cast off 8sts, P1, C2L, K2, P2, (P1, K1) five times

Continue on to Left Front

Left Front: (Includes button band worked in moss stitch)

Wrong side facing, work on **first 18 sts** in Left Front Stitch Pattern I

Left Front Stitch Pattern I:

Row 1: (K1, P1) five times, K2, P4, K2

Row 2: P2, K1, C2L, K1, P2, (P1, K1) five times

Row 3: as row 1

Row 4: P2, K2, C2L, P2, (P1, K1) five times

Row 5: as row 1

Row 6: P2, C2L, K2, P2, (P1, K1) five times

These six rows form the pattern stitch

Continue as follows:

Rows 7 – 12: Repeat rows 1 – 6, **one more time**

Continue on to Neck Shaping

Cardigan ~ Bria Collection Cont

Neck Shaping:

Wrong side facing, work as follows:

Row 1: (K1, P1) five times K2tog, P4, K2

Row 2: P2, K1, C2L, K1, P1, (P1, K1) five times

Row 3: (K1, P1) five times, P2tog, P3, K2 = *16 sts*

Continue on in Left Front Stitch Pattern II

Left Front Stitch Pattern II:

Row 1: P2, K3, P1, (P1, K1) five times

Row 2: (K1, P1) five times, K1, P3, K2

These two rows form the pattern stitch

Continue as follows:

Rows 3 – 10: Repeat rows 1 – 2, **four more times**

Continue on to Shape Shoulder

Shape Shoulder:

Next Row: Cast off 7sts, (P1, K1) four times

Continue working remaining 9sts for Shawl Collar

Shawl Collar:

Work in Shawl Collar Stitch Pattern

Shawl Collar Stitch Pattern:

Row 1: * K1, P1, rep from * to last st; K1

Row 2: K1, * P1, K1, rep from * to end

These two rows form the **moss stitch** pattern

Continue as follows:

Rows 3 – 20: Repeat rows 1 – 2, **nine more times**

Cast off loosely in pattern.

Continue on to Back

Cardigan ~ Bria Collection

Back:

Wrong side facing, rejoin yarn to **center 26 sts,** work in Back Stitch Pattern

Back Stitch Pattern:

Row 1: P2, K2, * K1, P1, rep from * to last 4 sts; K2, P2

Row 2: K2, P2, * P1, K1, rep from * to last 4 sts; P2, K2

These two rows form the pattern stitch

Continue as follows:

Rows 3 – 21: Repeat rows 1 – 2, **nine more times,** then work **row 1** *only*, **once more**

Continue on to Shape Shoulders

Shape Shoulders:

Next Row: Cast off 7sts, * P1, K1, rep from * to last 4 sts; P2, K2

Next Row: Cast off 7 sts, * K1, P1, rep from * to last st; K1

Cast off loosely in pattern

Continue on to Right Front

Right Front: (Includes button band worked in moss stitch)

Wrong side facing, work on **remaining 18 sts** in Right Front Stitch Pattern I

Right Front Stitch Pattern I:

Row 1: K2, P4, K2, * K1, P1, rep from * to end

Row 2: (P1, K1) five times, P2, K1, C2L, K1, P2

Row 3: as row 1

Row 4: (P1, K1) five times, P2, K2, C2L, P2

Row 5: as row 1

Row 6: (3rd buttonholes) P1, K1, YO, K2tog, (P1, K1) two times, YO, K2tog, P2, C2L, K2, P2

These six rows form the pattern stitch

Continue as follows:

Row 7: as row 1

Rows 8 – 11: Repeat rows 2 – 5, **once more**

Row 12: (P1, K1) five times, P2, C2L, K2, P2

Continue on to Neck Shaping

Cardigan ~ Bria Collection Cont

Neck Shaping:

Wrong side facing, work as follows:

Row 1: K2, P4, K2tog, * K1, P1, rep from * to end

Row 2: (P1, K1) five times, P1, K1, C2L, K1, P2

Row 3: K2, P3, P2tog, * K1, P1, rep from * to end = *16 sts*

Row 4: (P1, K1) five times K2, C2L, P2

Continue on in Right Front Stitch Pattern II

Right Front Stitch Pattern II:

Row 1: K2, P4, * K1, P1, rep from * to end

Row 2: (P1, K1) five times, K4, P2

These two rows form the pattern stitch

Continue as follows:

Rows 3 – 8: Repeat rows 1 – 2, **three more times**

Continue on to Shape Shoulder

Shape Shoulder:

Next Row: Cast off 7sts, * K1, P1, rep from * to end

Continue on to work Shawl Collar

Shawl Collar:

Work in Shawl Collar Stitch Pattern

Shawl Collar Stitch Pattern:

Row 1: P1, * K1, P1, rep from * to end

Row 2: * P1, K1, rep from * to last st; P1

These two rows continue the **moss stitch** pattern for collar

Continue as follows:

Rows 3 – 20: Repeat rows 1 – 2, **nine more times**

Cast off loosely in pattern

Continue on to Complete Collar

Cardigan ~ Bria Collection Cont

Complete Collar: Right sides facing, sew shoulder seams, sew cast off edges of collar together, align this collar seam to center back and sew in place across back. Weave in yarn breaks.

Continue on to work **Sleeves** as given for sweater see pg 17

Completed Cardigan Measurement: approx. 6 ½" from cast on edge to shoulder seam, with a sleeve length of approx. 6" from cuff edge to top of sleeve cap.

6 ½"

6"

- 24 -

by Debonair Designs ~ copyright © 2011 - 2013 Debonair Designs

Newsboy Cap ~ Bria Collection

Pattern Features: The pattern has been written out with line-by-line instructions given along with variations for working contrast color

Construction: Worked flat: Back and forth in rows, from the brim to crown in one piece then seamed. Cap peak worked separately then sewn in place

Materials: 65 – 70 yards (1 – 2 ¼ ounces) of worsted weight yarn, including scraps of used for contrast

Knitting Needles: Pair of 3.25mm throughout (US 3-UK/CANADIAN 10)

Notions: 1 Button size ½" (12mm) used for decoration on top of crown, Darning Needle

Gauge: Using 3.25mm needles: 6 sts and 7 rows in 1in over stockinette stitch

Skill Level:

BEGINNER   EASY

Main Body:

Begin at brim edge, **cast on 46sts** *loosely,* work as follows:

Rows 1 – 2: Work in **garter stitch**

(Variation: work these two rows in contrast color)

Continue as follows:

Rows 3 – 4: Beginning with a <u>knit row,</u> work in stockinette stitch

Row 5: (inc) K1, * kfb in next st, rep from * to last stitch; K1 = *90 sts*

Rows 6 – 8: Beginning with a **purl row,** work in stockinette stitch

Row 9: (inc) * K8, kfb in next 2 sts, rep from * to end = *108 sts*

Rows 10 – 14: Beginning with a **purl row,** work in stockinette stitch

Row 15: (dec) * K8, K2tog, K2tog, rep from * to end = *90 sts*

Row 16: P across all sts

Continue on to Crown

Newsboy Cap ~ Bria Collection

Crown:

Row 1: (dec right side) * K8, K2tog, rep from * to end = *81 sts*

Rows 2, 4, 6, 8, 10, 12, 14: P across all sts

Row 3: (dec) * K7, K2tog, rep from * to end = *72 sts*

Row 5: (dec) * K6, K2tog, rep from * to end = *63 sts*

Row 7: (dec) * K5, K2tog, rep from * to end = *54 sts*

Row 9: (dec) * K4, K2tog, rep from * to end = *45 sts*

Row 11: (dec) * K3, K2tog, rep from * to end = *36 sts*

Row 13: (dec) * K2, K2tog, rep from * to end = *27 sts*

Row 15: (dec) * K1, K2tog, rep from * to end = *18 sts*

Row 16: (dec) * P2tog; rep from * to end = *9 sts*

Break yarn and thread through remaining stitches, drawing up firmly and fasten securely. Join seam.

Continue on to Cap Peak

Cap Peak:

Beginning at inner edge, **cast on 20 sts**

(Variation: cast on using a contrast color working rows 1 - 3)

Row 1: (inc) K2 * kfb in next st, K2, rep from * to end = *26 sts*

Rows 2 – 3: Beginning with a **purl row,** work in **stockinette stitch**

(Variation: change to main color if contrast was used prior)

Row 4: (wrong side) K across all sts to mark outer edge fold line

Rows 5 – 6: Beginning with a **knit row,** work in **stockinette stitch**

Row 7: (dec) K2, * K2tog, K2, rep from * to end = *20 sts*

Cast off remaining sts, continue on to Complete

Complete: Gather up each set of row ends and fasten off. Right sides together, sew cast on and cast off edges together. Sew this edge to the garter stitch edge of cap's main piece at center front. Sew on button at top of crown. **Completed Measurements:** Designed to fit head circumference of 13" (33cm) approx.

Irish Warmer ~ Bria Collection

Model wearing **Irish Warmer** paired with **Newsboy Cap**

Pattern Features: The pattern has been written out with line-by-line instructions given, including buttonhole placement. Set in long sleeves and turtle-neck created from picked up stitches.

Construction: Worked flat: Back and forth in rows, from bottom up in one piece to armholes, then each section is worked individually

Materials: 210 – 230 yards (4 - 4 ¾ ounces) of worsted or aran weight yarn

Knitting Needles: Pair of 3.75mm throughout (US 5-UK/CANADIAN 9)

Notions: 6 Buttons size 9/16" (13mm), Darning Needle, 2 Stitch Holders or Safety Pins

Gauge: Using 3.75mm needles: 6 sts and 7 rows in 1in over Moss Knit Rib Stitch

Skill Level: EASY / INTERMEDIATE

Main Body: (Includes 3 sts worked in garter stitch at each end for button bands indicated in *italics*)

Begin at lower edge, **cast on 74 sts**, work in Stitch Pattern

Stitch Pattern:

Row 1: (right side) *K3,* * K3, P1, rep from * to last 3 sts; *K3*

Row 2: *K3,* * K2, P1, K1, rep from * to last 3 sts; *K3*

These two rows form the pattern stitch

Continue as follows:

Row 3: (1st buttonhole) *K3,* * K3, P1, rep from * to last 3 sts; *K1, YO, K2tog*

Row 4: as row 2

Rows 5 – 12: Repeat rows 1 – 2, **four more times**

Row 13: (2nd buttonhole) as row 3

Row 14: as row 2

Rows 15 – 22: Repeat rows 1 – 2, **four more times**

Row 23: (3rd buttonhole) as row 3

Row 24: as row 2

Rows 25 – 28: Repeat rows 1 – 2, **two more times**

Continue on to Divide

Irish Warmer ~ Bria Collection Cont

Divide:

Next Row: *K3,* (K3, P1) three times, K2, cast off 8 sts, P1, (K3, P1) five times, K2, cast off 8 sts, P1, (K3, P1) three times, *K3*

Continue on to Right Back

Right Back: (Includes 3 sts worked in garter stitch for button band indicated in *italics*)

Wrong side facing, work on **first 17 sts** in Right Back Stitch Pattern

Right Back Stitch Pattern:

Row 1: *K3,* * K2, P1, K1, rep from * to last 2 sts; K2

Row 2: K1, P1, * K3, P1, rep from * to last 3 sts; *K3*

These two rows form the pattern stitch

Continue as follows:

Row 3: as row 1

Row 4: (4th buttonhole) K1, P1, * K3, P1, rep from * to last 3 sts; *K1, YO, K2tog*

Rows 5 – 13: Repeat rows 1 – 2, **four more times**, then work **row 1** *only*, **once more**

Row 14: (5th buttonhole) as row 4

Rows 15 – 19: Repeat rows 1 – 2, **two more times**, then work **row 1** *only*, **once more**

Continue on to Shape Shoulder

Shape Shoulder:

Next Row: Cast off 8 sts, P1, K3, P1, *K3*

Next Row: *K3,* K2, P1, K3

Next Row: Cast off 6 sts, K to end (place remaining 3sts on stitch holder or safety pin)

Continue on to Front

SEASONAL HAND KNITTED DESIGNS FOR 18" DOLLS ~ SPRING/SUMMER COLLECTION

Irish Warmer ~ Bria Collection

Front:

Wrong side facing, rejoin yarn to **center 24 sts**, work in Front Stitch Pattern

Front Stitch Pattern:

Row 1: P1, K1, * K2, P1, K1, rep from * to last 2 sts; K2

Row 2: K1, P1, * K3, P1, rep from * to last 2 sts; K2

These two rows form the pattern stitch

Continue as follows:

Rows 3 – 13: Repeat rows 1 – 2, **five more times,** then work **row 1** *only,* once more

Continue on to Neck Shaping

Neck Shaping:

Row 1: K1, P1, (K3, P1) two times, K2tog, *turn*

Row 2: K2tog, K1, P1, K3, P1, K3

Row 3: K1, P1, K3, P1, K2, K2tog, *turn*

Row 4: P2tog, K3, P1, K3 = *8 sts*

Row 5: K1, P1, K3, P1, K2, *turn*

Cast off remaining sts for shoulder, right side facing, rejoin yarn to remaining sts, work as follows:

Row 1: K2tog, (K3, P1) two times, K2

Row 2: P1, (K3, P1) two times, K2tog

Row 3: K2tog, K1, P1, K3, P1, K2

Row 4: P1, K3, P1, K2, K2tog = *8 sts*

Row 5: K1, P1, K3, P1, K2

Cast off remaining sts for shoulder, continue on to Left Back

Irish Warmer ~ Bria Collection

Left Back: (Includes 3 sts worked in garter stitch for button band indicated in *italics*)

Wrong side facing, rejoin yarn to **remaining 17 sts** work in Left Back Stitch Pattern

Left Back Stitch Pattern:

Row 1: P1, K1, * K2, P1, K1, rep from * to last 3 sts; *K3*

Row 2: *K3,* * K3, P1, rep from * to last 2 sts; K2

These two rows form the pattern stitch
Continue as follows:

Rows 3 – 18: Repeat rows 1 – 2, **eight more times**

Continue on to Shape Shoulder

Shape Shoulder:

Next Row: Cast off 8 sts, K3, P1, K1, K3

Next Row: K3, K3, P1, K2

Next Row: Cast off 6 sts, K to end
(place remaining 3sts on stitch holder or safety pin)
Continue on to Turtle-Neck

Right sides together join shoulder seams

Turtle-Neck: (Includes 3 sts worked in garter stitch at each end for button bands indicated in *italics*)

Right side facing rejoin yarn to 3 sts held for button band; *K3,* pick up and knit; 7 sts across right back, 2 sts across seam, 7 sts along right side of neckline, 7 sts along left side of neckline, 2 sts across seam, 7 sts across left back, *K3,* from second set of button band sts on hold = *38 sts*

Continue in Turtle-Neck Stitch Pattern

Irish Warmer ~ Bria Collection Cont

Turtle-Neck Stitch Pattern:

Row 1: *K3,* **P1, K1, rep from** * **to last 3 sts;** *K3*

Row 2: (top 6th buttonhole) *K3,* **P1, K1, rep from** * **to last 3 sts;** *K1, YO, K2tog*

These two rows form the pattern stitch

Continue as follows:

Rows 3 – 5: Repeat row 1, **three more times**

Cast off all sts loosely in pattern

Continue on to Sleeves

Sleeves: Both alike

Sleeve Tip: refer to pg 10

Begin at cuff edge, **cast on 23 sts,** work in Cuff Stitch Pattern

Cuff Stitch Pattern:

Rows 1 – 4: Work in **single ribbing**

Row 5: (inc) K6, kfb in next 11 sts, K6 = *34 sts*

Row 6: (wrong side) K across all sts

These six rows **complete** the cuff

Continue on to Sleeve Stitch Pattern

Sleeve Stitch Pattern:

Row 1: P1, * K3, P1, rep from * to last st; K1

Row 2: K1, * K2, P1, K1, rep from * to last st; K1

These two rows form the pattern stitch

Continue as follows:

Rows 3 – 24: Repeat rows 1 – 2, **eleven more times**

Continue on to Shape Sleeve Top

Irish Warmer ~ Bria Collection Cont

Shaping Tip: refer to pg 10

Shape Sleeve Top:

Right side facing, work as follows:

Row 1: Cast off 3 sts, P1, * K3, P1, rep from * to last st; K1

Row 2: Cast off 3 sts, * K3, P1, rep from * to last 3 sts; K3

Row 3: Cast off 3 sts, K1, P1, * K3, P1, rep from * to last 2 sts; K2

Row 4: Cast off 3 sts, P1, * K3, P1, rep from * to end

Row 5: Cast off 3 sts, * K2, P1, K1; rep from * to last 2 sts; K2

Row 6: Cast off 3 sts, * P2tog; rep from * to last st; P1 = *9 sts*

Cast off remaining sts

Continue on to **Complete**

Complete: Right sides together, join sleeve seams to beginning of sleeve top shaping. Wrong side facing, insert to cast off stitches of armhole opening, sew evenly around opening. Sew on buttons.

Completed Measurements: approx. 6" from cast on edge to shoulder seam, with a sleeve length of approx. 5 ¼" from cuff edge to top of sleeve cap.

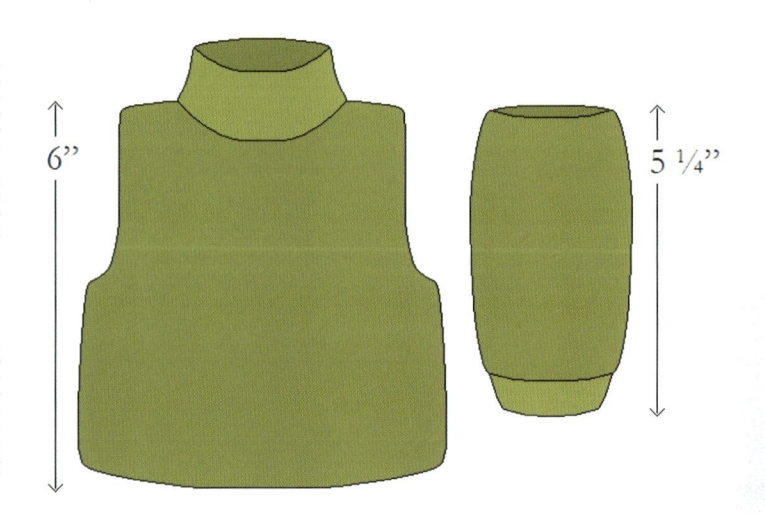

Of the Earth

Of the Earth Collection ~
Abbreviations & Tips

Standard Abbreviations:

Refer to pg viii

Special Abbreviations:

yb = yarn back (move yarn at back of work)

yf = yarn forward: This term is used in place of the words *yarn in front*, to do this, slip the yarn between the two needles bringing it forward, in this position the knitting can continue as stated

Color Key:

MC = main color, **A** = first contrast color

B = second contrast color

Stitch Patterns:

Seed Stitch = knit 1, purl 1, knit 1 every row

Stockinette Stitch = knit a row, purl a row

Seed Stitch Ribbing = see pattern

Tip for Sleeves: Cast on stitches for each sleeve on the same needle, using separate skeins for each sleeve, and working them at the same time

Tip for Sleeve Top Shaping: When working the cast off stitches over several rows as indicated, slip the first of the cast off stitches, then proceed with cast off, this makes for a smoother transition

Pattern Tip: When working the main color at each end for the button bands, I like to make use of two skeins, one for each end along with scraps of the contrast color. Be sure to wrap the contrast with the main color before working the seed stitch button bands to avoid gaps in color work

Pattern Clarification: Faux Fair Isle is an easy slipped stitch pattern that gives a Fair Isle look without the need for experience in colorwork, making use of slipped stitches where indicated in colors stated, whereas traditional Fair Isle is the technique often used to describe colorwork or stranded knitting where stitches are knit alternately in various colors, with the unused colors stranded across the back of the work

Pattern Note: Worked flat: Back and forth in rows

Construction: Refer to individual pattern pages for details

Skill Level: Refer to individual pattern pages for details

Materials: Refer to individual pattern pages for quantities

Worsted/10ply yarn used throughout
Yarn Equivalent: 8 ply, Aran (UK)

OF THE EARTH COLLECTION

~ 1 ~
Of the Earth Collection

Inspired by my love of fair isle stitch patterns and in keeping with today's fashion styles, shaped this ensemble, that makes use of slipped stitches to create the faux fair isle pattern without the need for experience in colorwork. A perfect addition to your doll's early spring wardrobe; stylish yet warm to celebrate the anticipated arrival of spring.

~ Debonair Designs

~ . ~ . ~ . ~

Model wearing **Ayanna** paired with **Pippi II**

Of the Earth Collection Patterns:

Ayanna ~ a faux fair isle stitched turtle-neck sweater dress .... Pg 36

Pippi II ~ a pair of matching faux fair isle stitched leg warmers .... Pg 45

Ayanna ~ Of the Earth Collection

Pattern Features: The faux fair isle is achieved with the use of slipped stitches, thereby avoiding the traditional stranded color work, written out with line-by-line instructions given, including back buttonhole placement. Set in ¾ length sleeves with a deep ribbed cuff and a ribbed stitched turtle-neck worked from picked up stitches complete the look.

Construction: Worked flat: Back and forth in rows, from the bottom up in one piece to armholes, then each section is worked individually

Materials: 190 – 200 yards (3 ¾ – 4 ounces) of worsted or aran weight yarn including scraps worked for contrast A & B

Knitting Needles: Pair of 3.25mm throughout (US 3-UK/CANADIAN 10)

Notions: 6 Buttons size ½" (12mm), Darning Needle, 2 Stitch Holders or Safety Pins

Gauge: Using 3.25mm needles: 6 sts and 7 rows in 1in over seed stitch ribbing

Skill Level: EASY

Welt: (Includes 3 sts worked in seed stitch at each end for button bands indicated in *italics*)

Color Key: MC = main color

With MC, begin at lower edge **cast on 83 sts,** work in Seed Stitch Ribbing Pattern

Seed Stitch Ribbing Pattern:

Row 1: (right side) *K1, P1, K1,* * *P2, K1, P1, K1, rep from * to last 5 sts; P2, K1, P1, K1*

Row 2: *K1, P1, K1, K2,* * *P3, K2, rep from * to last 3 sts; K1, P1, K1*

These two rows form the pattern stitch

Continue as follows:

Rows 3 – 4: Repeat rows 1 – 2, **one more time**

Row 5: (1st buttonhole) *K1, P1, K1,* * *P2, K1, P1, K1, rep from * to last 5 sts; P2, K1, YO, K2tog*

Row 6: as row 2

Rows 7 – 14: Repeat rows 1 – 2, **four more times**

Row 15: (dec) *K1, P1, K1,* K2tog, K to last 5 sts; K2tog, *K1, P1, K1* = *81 sts*

Continue onto Main Body

Ayanna ~ Of the Earth Collection

Main Body: (Includes 3 sts worked in seed stitch at each end for button bands indicated in *italics*)

Pattern Note: All slip stitches are slipped purlwise
Color Key: **MC** = main color **A** = first contrast color
B = second contrast color

Continue and work in Faux Fair Isle Pattern

Faux Fair Isle Pattern:
Pattern Tip: refer to pg 34

Row 1: (wrong side) Using MC, *K1, P1, K1,* P1, yb, sl1, yf, * P3, yb, sl1, yf, rep from * to last 4 sts; P1, *K1, P1, K1*

Row 2: Using MC, *K1, P1, K1,* K1, * sl1, K3, rep from * to last 5 sts; sl1, K1, *K1, P1, K1*

Row 3: *Using MC, K1, P1, K1, (join on A),* using A, P3, * yb, sl1, yf, P3, rep from * to last 3 sts; *(join on 2nd skein of MC), using MC, K1, P1, K1*

Row 4: *Using MC, K1, P1, K1,* using A, * K3, sl1, rep from * to last 6 sts; K3, *using MC, K1, P1, K1*

These four rows form the pattern stitch

Continue as follows:

Row 5: *Using MC, K1, P1, K1, (join on B),* using B, P1, yb sl1 yf, * P3, yb, sl1, yf, rep from * to last 4 sts; P1, *using MC, K1, P1, K1*

Row 6: *Using MC, K1, P1, K1,* using B, K1, * sl1, K3, rep from * to last 5 sts; sl1, K1, *using MC, K1, P1, K1 break B*

Rows 7 – 8: Repeat rows 3 – 4, **once more** *break A*

Rows 9 – 10: Repeat rows 1 – 2, **once more**

Row 11: Using MC, *K1, P1, K1,* P3, * yb, sl1, yf, P3, rep from * to last 3 sts; *K1, P1, K1*

Row 12: (2nd buttonhole) Using MC, *K1, P1, K1,* * K3, sl1, rep from * to last 6 sts; K3, *K1, YO, K2tog*

Rows 13 – 21: Repeat rows 1 – 4, **two more times,** then work **row 1** *only,* **once more**

Row 22: (dec) Using MC, *K1, P1, K1,* K12, K2tog, K1, K2tog, K to last 20 sts; K2tog, K1, K2tog, K12, *K1, P1, K1 = 77 sts*

Row 23: as row 11

Row 24: (3rd buttonhole) as row 12

Row 25: *Using MC, K1, P1, K1, (join on A),* using A, P1, yb sl1 yf, * P3, yb, sl1, yf, rep from * to last 4 sts; P1, *using MC, K1, P1, K1*

Row 26: *Using MC, K1, P1, K1,* using A, K1, * sl1, K3, rep from * to last 5 sts; sl1, K1, *using MC, K1, P1, K1*

Rows 27 – 28: Repeat rows 11 – 12, **once more** omit buttonhole, work seed stitch as established

Rows 29 – 30: Repeat rows 25 – 26, **once more** *break A*

Rows 31 – 32: Repeat rows 11 – 12, **once more** omit buttonhole, work seed stitch as established

Rows 33 – 34: Repeat rows 1 – 2, **once more**

Row 35: as row 11

Continue on to Divide

Ayanna ~ Of the Earth Collection Cont

Divide:

Next Row: (4th buttonhole) Using MC, *K1, P1, K1,* K14, cast off 8 sts, K until there are 27sts on right-hand needle, cast off 8 sts, K to last 3 sts; *K1, YO, K2tog*

Continue on to Right Back

Right Back: (Includes 3 sts worked in seed stitch for button band indicated in *italics*)

Color Key: **MC** = main color **A** = first contrast color **B** = second contrast color

Wrong side facing, work on **first 17 sts** in Right Back Faux Fair Isle Pattern

Right Back Faux Fair Isle Pattern:

Row 1: *Using MC, K1, P1, K1,* (join on A), using A, P1, yb, sl1, yf, * P3, yb, sl1, yf, rep from * to end

Row 2: Using A, * sl1, K3, rep from * to last 5 sts; sl1, K1, *using MC, K1, P1, K1*

Row 3: *Using MC, K1, P1, K1,* (join on B), using B, P3, * yb, sl1, yf, P3, rep from * to last 3 sts; yb, sl1, yf, P2

Row 4: Using B, K2, sl1, * K3, sl1, rep from * to last 6 sts; K3, *using MC, K1, P1, K1 break B*

These four rows form the pattern stitch

Continue as follows:

Rows 5 – 6: Repeat rows 1 – 2, **once more** *break A*

Row 7: Using MC, *K1, P1, K1,* P3, * yb, sl1, yf, P3, rep from * to last 3 sts; yb, sl1, yf, P2

Row 8: Using MC, K2, sl1, * K3, sl1, rep from * to last 6 sts; K3, *K1, P1, K1*

Using MC, continue on to Stitch Pattern II

Ayanna ~ Of the Earth Collection Cont

Stitch Pattern II:

Row 1: *K1, P1, K1, P to end*

Row 2: *K to last 3 sts; K1, P1, K1*

These two rows form the pattern stitch

Continue as follows:

Row 3: as row 1

Row 4: (5th buttonhole) *K to last 3 sts; K1, YO, K2tog*

Rows 5 – 13: Repeat rows 1 – 2, **four more times,** then work **row 1** *only*, once more

Continue on to Shape Shoulder

Shape Shoulder:

Next Row: Cast off 8 sts, *K to last 3 sts; K1, P1, K1*

Next Row: *K1, P1, K1, P to end*
(place these 9 sts on stitch holder or safety pin)

Continue on to Front

Front:

Color Key: MC = main color **A** = first contrast color
B = second contrast color

Wrong side facing, join on A to **center 27 sts,** work in Front Faux Fair Isle Pattern

Front Faux Fair Isle Pattern:

Row 1: Using A, P1, yb, sl1, yf, * P3, yb sl1, yf, rep from * to last st; P1

Row 2: Using A, K1, * sl1, K3, rep from * to last 2 sts; sl1, K1

Row 3: (Join on B), using B, P3, * yb, sl1, yf, P3, rep from * to end

Row 4: Using B, * K3, sl1, rep from * to last 3 sts; K3 *break B*

These four rows form the pattern stitch

Continue as follows:

Rows 5 – 6: Repeat rows 1 – 2**, once more** *break A*

Row 7: (Join on MC), using MC, P3, * yb, sl1, yf, P3, rep from * to end

Row 8: Using MC, * K3, sl1, rep from * to last 3 sts; K3

Using MC, continue as follows:

Rows 9 – 11: Beginning with a **purl row** work in **stockinette stitch**

Continue on to Neck Shaping

Ayanna ~ Of the Earth Collection Cont

Neck Shaping:

Right side facing, work as follows:

Row 1: K12, K2tog, *turn*

Row 2: P2tog, P to end

Row 3: K10, K2tog *turn*

Row 4: as row 2

Row 5: K8, K2tog *turn*

Row 6: as row 2 = *8 sts*

Row 7: K8, *turn*

Row 8: P to end

Cast off remaining sts for shoulder, cont as follows:

Right side facing, rejoin MC to remaining sts, work as follows:

Row 1: K to end

Row 2: P to last 2 sts; P2tog

Row 3: K2tog, K to end

Row 4: as row 2

Row 5: as row 3

Row 6: as row 2 = *8 sts*

Row 7: as row 1

Row 8: P to end

Cast off remaining sts for shoulder

Continue on to Left Back

Ayanna ~ Of the Earth Collection

Left Back: (Includes 3 sts worked in seed stitch for button band indicated in *italics*)

Color Key: MC = main color **A** = first contrast color
B = second contrast color

Wrong side facing, join on A to **remaining 17 sts,** work in Left Back Faux Fair Isle Pattern

Left Back Faux Fair Isle Pattern:

Row 1: Using A, P1, yb, sl1, yf, * P3, yb, sl1, yf, rep from * to last 3 sts; (join on MC), *using MC, K1, P1, K1*

Row 2: *Using MC, K1, P1, K1* using A, * sl1, K3, rep from * to last 2 sts; sl1, K1

Row 3: (Join on B), using B, P3, * yb, sl1, yf, P3, rep from * to last 6 sts; yb, sl1, yf, P2, *using MC, K1, P1, K1*

Row 4: *Using MC, K1, P1, K1* using B, K2, sl1, * K3, sl1, rep from * to last 3 sts; K3 *break B*

These four rows form the pattern stitch

Continue as follows:

Rows 5 – 6: Repeat rows 1 – 2, **once more** *break A*

Row 7: (Join on extra length of MC), using MC, P3, * yb, sl1, yf, P3, rep from * to last 6 sts; yb, sl1, yf, P2, *K1, P1, K1 break extra length of MC*

Row 8: Using MC, *K1, P1, K1,* K2, sl1, * K3, sl1, rep from * to last 3 sts; K3

Using MC, continue on to Stitch Pattern II

Stitch Pattern II:

Row 1: P to last 3 sts; *K1, P1, K1*

Row 2: *K1, P1, K1,* K to end

These two rows form the pattern stitch

Continue as follows:

Rows 3 – 14: Repeat rows 1 – 2, **six more times**

Continue on to Shape Shoulder

Ayanna ~ **Of the Earth Collection** Cont

Shape Shoulder:

Next Row: Cast off 8 sts, P to last 3 sts; *K1, P1, K1* (place remaining 9 sts on stitch holder or safety pin)

Right sides together, join shoulder seams

Continue on to Turtle Neck

Turtle-Neck: (Includes 3 sts worked in seed stitch at each end for button bands indicated in *italics*)

Right side facing, rejoin MC to 9 sts held *K1, P1, K1,* K2, P2, K2, pick up and knit 2 sts across shoulder seam, 11 sts along left side of neckline, 11 sts along right side of neckline, 2 sts across shoulder seam, place 9 sts held on to second needle and; K2, P2, K2, *K1, P1, K1 = 44 sts*

Continue in Turtle-Neck Stitch Pattern

Turtle-Neck Stitch Pattern:

Row 1: *K1, P1, K1,* * P2, K2, rep from * to last 5 sts; P2, *K1, P1, K1*

Row 2: (top 6th buttonhole) *K1, P1, K1,* K2, * P2, K2, rep from * to last 3 sts; *K1, YO, K2tog*

These two rows form the pattern stitch

Continue as follows:

Rows 3 – 16: Repeat rows 1 – 2, **seven more times,** omit buttonhole work seed stitch as established.

Cast off all sts loosely in pattern

Continue on to Sleeves

Model wearing **Ayanna** paired with **Belle** from the Neapolitan Chic Collection (pg 49)

Sleeves: Both alike

Pattern Note: all slip stitches are slipped purlwise
Sleeve Tip: refer to pg 34

With MC, begin at cuff edge **cast on 22 sts,** work Cuff Stitch Pattern

Cuff Stitch Pattern:

Row 1: (right side) * P2, K1, P1, K1, rep from * to last 2 sts; P2

Row 2: K2, * P3, K2, rep from * to end

These two rows form the pattern stitch
Continue as follows:

Rows 3 – 14: Repeat rows 1 – 2, **six more times**

Row 15: (inc) K5, kfb in next 13 sts, K4 = *35 sts*

These fifteen rows **complete** the cuff

Continue on to Faux Fair Isle Pattern

Ayanna ~ Of the Earth Collection Cont

Faux Fair Isle Pattern:

Row 1: (wrong side) (Join on A), using A, P1, yb, sl1, yf, * P3, yb, sl1, yf, rep from * to last st; P1

Row 2: Using A, K1, * sl1, K3, rep from * to last 2 sts; sl1, K1

Row 3: Using MC, P3, * yb, sl1, yf, P3, rep from * to end

Row 4: Using MC, * K3, sl1, rep from * to last 3 sts; K3

These four rows form the pattern stitch

Continue as follows:

Rows 5 – 8: Repeat rows 1 – 4, **one more time**

Row 9: Using MC, P1, yb, sl1, yf, * P3, yb, sl1, yf, rep from * to last st; P1

Row 10: Using MC, K1, * sl1, K3, rep from * to last 2 sts; sl1, K1

Rows 11 – 12: Repeat rows 3 – 4**, once more** *break MC*

Rows 13 – 14: Repeat rows 1 – 2**, once more**

Row 15: (Join on B), using B, P3, * yb, sl1, yf, P3, rep from * to end

Row 16: Using B, * K3, sl1, rep from * to last 3 sts; K3 *break B*

Continue on to Shape Sleeve Top

Shape Sleeve Top

Shaping Tip: refer to pg 34

Wrong side facing, work as follows:

Row 1: Using A, cast off 3 sts, P1, yb, sl1, yf, * P3, yb, sl1, yf, rep from * to last st; P1

Row 2: Using A, cast off 3 sts, K1, sl1, * K3, sl1, rep from * to last 2 sts; K2 *break A*

Row 3: (Join on MC), using MC, cast off 3 sts, * yb, sl1, yf, P3, rep from * to last st; P1

Continue in MC as follows:

Row 4: Cast off 3 sts, K to end

Row 5: Cast off 3 sts, P to end

Row 6: Cast off 3 sts, * K2tog, rep from * to end *= 9 sts*

Row 7: P to end

Cast off remaining 9 sts, continue on to Complete

- 43 -

by Debonair Designs ~ copyright © 2011 - 2013 Debonair Designs

SEASONAL HAND KNITTED DESIGNS FOR 18" DOLLS ~ SPRING/SUMMER COLLECTION

Ayanna ~ Of the Earth Collection Cont

Complete: Right sides together, join sleeve seams to beginning of sleeve top shaping. Wrong side facing, insert to cast off stitches of armhole opening, sew evenly around opening. Right side facing turn up cuff if desired. Sew on buttons. Fold down turtle neck.

Completed Measurements: approx. 8" from cast on edge to shoulder seam, with a sleeve length of approx. 3 ¾" from folded cuff edge to top of sleeve cap, 4 ¼" from unfolded cuff edge (as pictured) to top of sleeve cap.

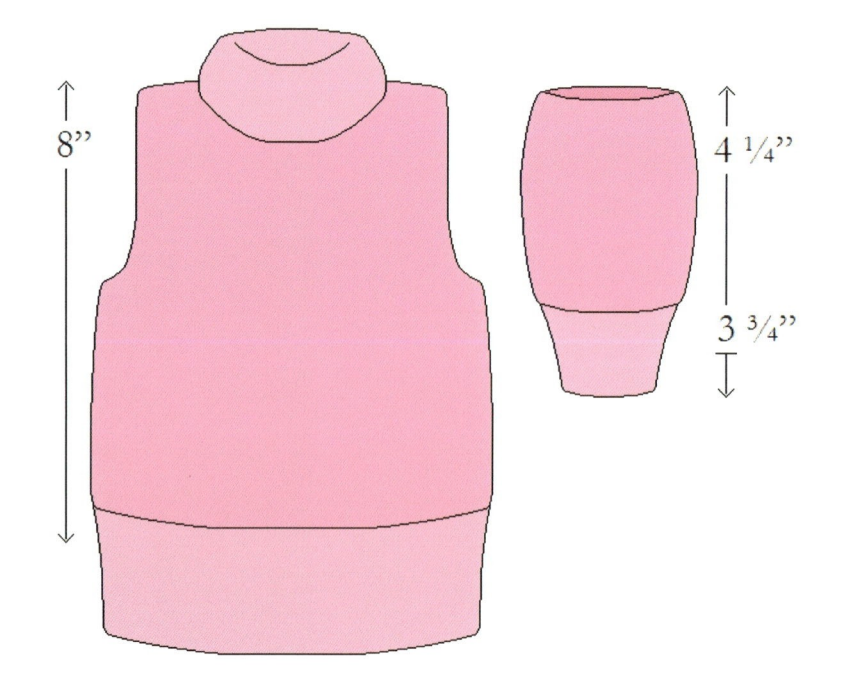

- 44 -

by Debonair Designs ~ copyright © 2011 - 2013 Debonair Designs

Pippi II ~ Of the Earth Collection

Pattern Features: The faux fair isle stitch pattern has been written out with line-by-line instructions given and achieved by the use of slipped stitches throughout

Construction: Worked flat: Back and forth in rows, from the bottom up in one piece with fold down cuff, then seamed

Materials: 25 – 30 yards (¾ ounce) of worsted weight yarn, including scraps worked for contrast A & B

Knitting Needles: Pair of 3.25mm throughout (US 3-UK/CANADIAN 10)

Notion: Darning Needle

Gauge: Using 3.25mm needles: 8 sts and 8 rows in 1in over single ribbing

Skill Level:

BEGINNER   EASY

Main Piece: (Both alike)

With MC, begin at lower edge **cast on 25 sts,** work in Cuff Stitch Pattern

Cuff Stitch Pattern

Row 1: (right side) * P2, K1, P1, K1, rep from * to end

Row 2: * P3, K2, rep from * to end

These two rows form the pattern stitch
Continue as follows:

Rows 3 – 5: Repeat rows 1 – 2, <u>one more time</u>, then work **row 1** *only,* <u>once more</u>
Continue and work in Faux Fair Isle Pattern

Pippi II ~ **Of the Earth Collection** Cont

Faux Fair Isle Pattern

Pattern Note: All slip stitches are slipped purlwise

Row 1: (wrong side) Using MC, P1, yb, sl1, yf, * P3, yb, sl1, yf, rep from * to last 3 sts; P3

Row 2: Using MC, * K3, sl1, rep from * to last st; K1

Row 3: Join on A, using A, P3, * yb, sl1, yf, P3, rep from * to last 2 sts; yb, sl1, yf, P1

Row 4: Using A, K1, * sl1, K3, rep from * to end

These four rows form the pattern stitch

Continue as follows:

Row 5: Join on B, using B, P1, yb, sl1, yf, * P3, yb, sl1, yf, rep from * to last 3 sts; P3

Row 6: Using B, * K3, sl1, rep from * to last st; K1
break B

Rows 7 – 8: Repeat rows 3 – 4, **once more**

Rows 9 – 10: Repeat rows 1 – 2, **once more**

Row 11: Using MC, P3, * yb, sl1, yf, P3, rep from * to last 2 sts; yb, sl1, yf, P1

Row 12: Using MC, K1, * sl1, K3, rep from * to end

Rows 13 – 20: Repeat rows 1 – 4, **two more times**
break A

Row 21: as row 1

Using MC, continue on to **Top Cuff Stitch Pattern**

Top Cuff Stitch Pattern

Row 1: (right side) * P2, K1, P1, K1, rep from * to end

Row 2: * P3, K2, rep from * to end

These two rows form the pattern stitch

Continue as follows:

Rows 3 – 14: Repeat rows 1 – 2, **six more times**

Cast off loosely in pattern

Continue on to **Complete**

Complete: Right sides together, sew seam to beginning of top cuff pattern, turn right side out and complete seam, turn down top cuff (as pictured).

Neapolitan Chic

Neapolitan Chic Collection ~
Abbreviations & Tips

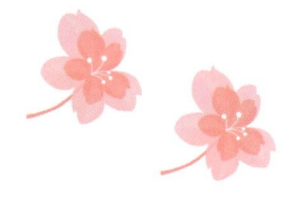

Standard Abbreviations:

Refer to pg viii

Special Abbreviations:

Cabana

Lateral Braid: * Knit into the back of the second stitch on the left hand needle, without sliding that stitch off, knit into the front of the first stitch, letting both first and second stitches slip off the left hand needle. Slip the first stitch on the right hand needle back on to the left hand needle and repeat from * to end of row *(A little tricky at first, but with patience, easily mastered)*

Kimana

ssk = slip the first stitch as if to knit, then slip the next stitch as if to knit. Insert the left needle into the front of both slipped stitches and knit them together, this produces a left slanting decrease

P3tog = purl 3 stitches together

Tip for Sleeves: Cast on stitches for each sleeve on the same needle, using separate skeins for each sleeve, and working them at the same time

Sleeve Top Shaping: When working the cast off stitches over several rows as indicated, slip the first of the cast off stitches, then proceed with cast off, this makes for a smoother transition

Stitch Patterns:

Seed Stitch = knit 1, purl 1, knit 1 every row

Garter Stitch = knit every row

Single Ribbing = knit 1, purl 1 every row

Stockinette Stitch = knit a row, purl a row

Crocheted Chain Stitch:
as pictured →

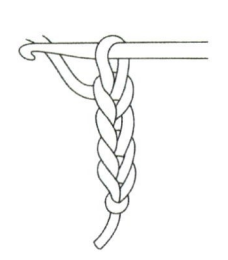

Pattern Note: Worked flat: Back and forth in rows

Construction: Refer to individual pattern pages for details

Skill Level: Refer to individual pattern pages for details

Materials: Refer to individual pattern pages for quantities

Worsted/10ply yarn used throughout
Yarn Equivalent: 8 ply, Aran (UK)

SEASONAL HAND KNITTED DESIGNS FOR 18" DOLLS ~ SPRING/SUMMER COLLECTION

NEAPOLITAN CHIC COLLECTION

~ 3 ~

Neapolitan Chic Collection

The Neapolitan Collection was born out of the desire to have various patterns working together for a complete outfit, this versatile collection comes with variations offering many color combinations to satisfy your creativity. Perfect for the spring into summer transition.
~ Debonair Designs

~.~.~.~.~

Neapolitan Chic Collection Patterns:

Cabana ~ a chevron stitched tunic top with additional petticoat skirt option . . . . . Pg 50

Kimana ~ a flattering bolero jacket . . . . Pg 57

Belle ~ a cloche style hat . . . . Pg 62

BoHoh ~ a ribbed stitched tote bag . . . . Pg 65

by Debonair Designs ~ copyright © 2011 - 2013 Debonair Designs

Cabana ~ Neapolitan Chic Collection

Models wearing **Cabana** paired with **Petticoat**

Pattern Features: The chevron stitch pattern has been written out with line-by-line instructions given, including back buttonhole placement, along with variations for working contrast color

Construction: Worked flat: Back and forth in rows, from bottom up in one piece to armholes, then each section is worked individually

Materials: 150 – 180 yards (3 – 3 ¾ ounces) of worsted weight yarn, including scraps used for contrast

Knitting Needles: Pair each of 3.25mm (US 3-UK/CANADIAN 10) and 3.75mm (US 5-UK/CANADIAN 9)

Notions: 5 Buttons size ½" (12mm), Darning Needle, Small Crochet Hook (size F) used for neckline at completion, Ribbon length for threading through eyelet row

Gauge: Using 3.75mm needles: 5 sts and 7 rows in 1in over chevron stitch

Skill Level:

EASY   INTERMEDIATE

Welt:

Using smaller sized needles, begin at lower edge, **cast on 85 sts,** work as follows:

(Variation: work these 4 rows in contrast color)

Row 1: (right side) P across all sts

Row 2: P across all sts

Row 3: Work Lateral Braid (instructions refer to pg 48)

Row 4: P across all sts

These four rows **complete** the welt

Continue on to Main Body

Cabana ~ Neapolitan Chic Collection

Main Body: (Includes 3 sts worked in seed stitch at each end for button bands indicated in *italics*)

Change to larger sized needles, work in **Stitch Pattern**

Stitch Pattern:

Row 1: (1st buttonhole) (right side) *K1, P1, K1,* * K1, YO, K4, K2tog, sl 1, K1, PSSO, K4, YO, rep from * to last 4 sts; *K1, K1, YO, K2tog*

Row 2: *K1, P1, K1,* P (including yarn overs) to last 3 sts; *K1, P1, K1*

These two rows form the stitch pattern

Continue as follows:

(Variation: work contrast color over first three pattern repeats)

Rows 3 – 10: Repeat rows 1 – 2, **four more times** omit buttonhole, work seed stitch as established

Row 11: (2nd buttonhole) as row 1

Row 12: as row 2

(Variation: work contrast color over last three pattern repeats)

Rows 13 – 20: Repeat rows 1 – 2, **four more times** omit buttonhole, work seed stitch as established

Row 21: (3rd buttonhole) as row 1

Row 22: as row 2

Rows 23 – 24: Repeat rows 1 – 2, **one more time,** omit buttonhole, work seed stitch as established

Row 25: (dec) *K1, P1, K1,* K2tog, K4, * K2tog, K11, rep from * to last 11 sts; K2tog K4, K2tog, *K1, P1, K1* = 77sts

Row 26: *K1, P1, K1,* P to last 3 sts; *K1, P1, K1*

Eyelet row featured at empire waistline with flower embellishments along neckline

Row 27: (eyelet row) *K1, P1, K1,* * YO, K2tog, rep from * to last 4 sts; K1, *K1, P1, K1*

Row 28: *K1, P1, K1,* P (including yarn overs) to last 3 sts; *K1, P1, K1*

Continue on to **Divide**

Divide:

Next Row: *K1, P1, K1,* K14, cast off 8 sts, K until there are 27sts on right-hand needle, cast off 8 sts, K to last 3 sts; *K1, P1, K1*

Continue on to **Right Back**

Cabana ~ Neapolitan Chic Collection

Right Back: (Includes 3 sts worked in seed stitch for button band indicated in *italics*)

Wrong side facing, work on **first 17 sts** as follows:

Next Row: *K1, P1, K1,* P to end

Continue and work in Right Back Stitch Pattern

Right Back Stitch Pattern:

Row 1: (4th buttonhole) P2, * K3, P1, rep from * to last 3 sts; *K1, YO, K2tog*

Row 2: *K1, P1, K1,* * K1, P3, rep from * to last 2sts; K2

These two rows form the stitch pattern

Continue as follows:

Rows 3 – 5: Repeat rows 1 – 2, **one more time**, then work **row 1 *only*, once more,** omit buttonhole, work seed stitch as established

Row 6: (wrong side) *K1, P1, K1,* K1, * P2tog, Yrn, P1, K1, rep from * to last st; K1

Rows 7 – 9: Repeat rows 1 – 2, **one more time**, then work **row 1 *only*, once more,** omit buttonhole, work seed stitch as established

Row 10: as row 6

Rows 11 – 12: Repeat rows 1 – 2, **one more time**, omit buttonhole, work seed stitch as established

Row 13: (5th buttonhole) as row 1

Row 14: as row 2

Rows 15 – 16: Repeat rows 1 – 2, **one more time**, omit buttonhole, work seed stitch as established

Continue on to Shape Shoulder

Shape Shoulder:

Next Row: Cast off 8 sts, P1, K3, P1, K1, P1, K1

Next Row: K1, P1, K1, K1, P3, K1, P1

Cast off remaining 9 sts

Continue on to Front

Front:

Wrong side facing, rejoin yarn to **center 27 sts**, work in Front Stitch Pattern

Front Stitch Pattern:

Row 1: K1, * K1, P3, rep from * to last 2 sts; K2

Row 2: K1, P1, * K3, P1, rep from * to last st; K1

These two rows form the stitch pattern

Continue as follows:

Rows 3 – 4: Repeat rows 1 – 2, **one more time**

Row 5: K2, * P2tog, Yrn, P1, K1, rep from * to last st; P1

Row 6: as row 2

Rows 7 – 8: Repeat rows 1 – 2, **one more time**

Row 9: as row 5

Continue on to Neck Shaping

Cabana ~ Neapolitan Chic Collection Cont

Neck Shaping:

Right side facing, work as follows:

Row 1: K1, P1, (K3, P1) two times, K2, K2tog *turn*

Row 2: P2tog, P1, (K1, P3) two times, K2

Row 3: K1, P1, (K3, P1) two times, K2tog, *turn*

Row 4: P2tog, (P3, K1) two times, K1

Row 5: K1, P1, K3, P1, K2, K2tog, *turn*

Row 6: P2tog, P1, K1, P3, K2 = *8 sts*

Row 7: K1, P1, K3, P1, K2 *turn*

Row 8: K3, P3, K2

Cast off remaining 8 sts for shoulder

Right side facing, rejoin yarn to remaining sts, work as follows:

Row 1: * K3, P1, rep from * to last st; K1

Row 2: K1, * K1, P3, rep from * to last 4 sts; K1, P1, P2tog

Row 3: K2tog, P1, * K3, P1, rep from * to last st; K1

Row 4: K1, * K1, P3, rep from * to last 2 sts; P2tog

Row 5: K2tog, K2, P1, K3, P1, K1

Row 6: K2, P3, K1, P1, P2tog = *8 sts*

Row 7: K2, P1 K3, P1, K1

Row 8: K2, P3, K1, P1, K1

Cast off remaining 8 sts for shoulder

Continue on to **Left Back**

Left Back: (Includes 3 sts worked in seed stitch for button band indicated in *italics*)

Wrong side facing, rejoin yarn to **remaining 17 sts,** work as follows:

Next Row: P to last 3 sts; *K1, P1, K1*

Continue and work in Left Back Stitch Pattern

Left Back Stitch Pattern:

Row 1: *K1, P1, K1,* * K3, P1, rep from * to last 2 sts; P2

Row 2: K2, * K1, P3, rep from * to last 3 sts; *K1, P1, K1*

These two rows form the stitch pattern

Continue as follows:

Rows 3 – 5: Repeat rows 1 – 2, **one more time,** then work **row 1** *only,* **once more**

Row 6: K3, * P2tog, YO, P1, K1, rep from * to last 6 sts; P2tog, YO, P1, *K1, P1, K1*

Rows 7 – 9: Repeat rows 1 – 2, **one more time,** then work **row 1** *only,* **once more**

Row 10: as row 6

Rows 11 – 17: Repeat rows 1 – 2, **three more times,** then work **row 1** *only,* **once more**

Continue on to Shape Shoulder

Shape Shoulder:

Next Row: (wrong side), cast off 8 sts, P1, K1, P3, *K1, P1, K1*

Cast off remaining 9 sts

Right sides together, join shoulder seams

Continue on to Neckline

Cabana ~ Neapolitan Chic Collection

Neckline: (Variation: work in contrast color)

Using a small crochet hook, work a chain stitch across entire neckline. **Tip:** refer to pg 48
Optional embellishment: work several knitted flowers and sew around neckline as follows: using small needles, **cast on 10 sts,** break yarn and thread back through the sts, pull tightly, catch row ends to form a circle, attach to neckline, use contrast for centers when sewing in place (as pictured ↓)

Continue on to Complete

Complete: Work a crocheted chain stitch around armholes. **Tip:** refer to pg 48 (Variation: work in contrast color). Thread ribbon choice through eyelet row and fasten to form a bow. Sew on buttons.

Bouquet worked from group of knitted flowers as worked at optional neckline finish, surrounded with lace and ribbon ties

Completed Measurements: approx. 7 ¼" from cast on edge to shoulder seam.

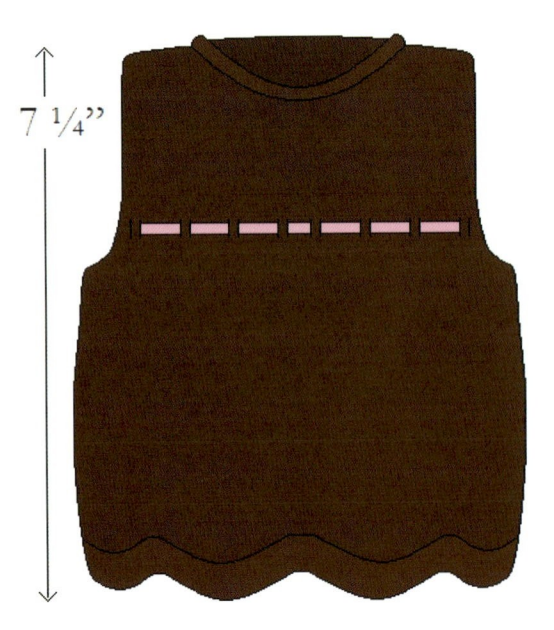

by Debonair Designs ~ copyright © 2011 - 2013 Debonair Designs

Cabana Petticoat Skirt ~ Neapolitan Chic Collection

Model wearing **Petticoat** paired with **Cabana**, **Belle** and **BoHoh**

Welt:

Using smaller sized needles, begin at lower edge, **cast on 85 sts,** work as follows:

(Variation: work these 4 rows in garter stitch and contrast)

Row 1: (right side) P across all sts

Row 2: P across all sts

Row 3: Work Lateral Braid (instructions refer to pg 48)

Row 4: P across all sts

These four rows **complete** the welt

Continue on to **Main Body**

Main Body:

Continue and work in Stitch Pattern

Stitch Pattern:

Row 1: (right side) K3, * K1, YO, K4, K2tog, sl 1, K1, PSSO, K4, YO, rep from * to last 4 sts; K4

Row 2: P (including yarn overs) to end

These two rows form the pattern stitch

(Variation: work these 2 rows in contrast)

Continue as follows:

Rows 3 – 18: Repeat rows 1 – 2, **eight more times**

(Variation: work one pattern repeat in contrast)

Row 19: (dec) K9, * K2tog, K11, rep from * to last 11 sts; K2tog, K5, K9 = *79 sts*

Row 20: as row 2

Row 21: (dec) K2, K2tog, * YO, K4, K2tog, sl 1, K1, PSSO, K3, YO, rep from * to last 3 sts; K2tog, K1 = *77 sts*

Row 22: as row 2

Rows 23: K3, * YO, K4, K2tog, sl 1, K1, PSSO, K3, YO, K1, rep from * to last 2 sts; K2

Row 24: as row 2

Rows 25 – 26: Work in **garter stitch**

Continue on to **Shape Waist**

Shape Waist:

Next Row: (dec) K1, K2tog, * K2, K2tog, rep from * to 2 sts, K2 = *58 sts*

Next Row: P (including yarn overs) to end

Continue on to **Waist Panel**

Cabana ~ Neapolitan Chic Collection Cont

Waist Panel:

Row 1: K across all sts

Row 2: K2, * P1, K1, rep from * to last 3 sts; P1, K2

These two rows form the pattern stitch

Continue as follows:

Rows 3 – 4: Repeat rows 1 – 2, **one more time**

Cast off all sts loosely, continue on to **Complete**

Complete: Right sides together, sew row ends from cast on sts to beginning of waist panel. Using a small crochet hook, chain stitch button loop to desired length.
Tip: refer to pg 48. Sew to left side edge of waist panel at back, sew button to correspond onto right side.

Completed Measurements: approx. 4 ½" from cast on edge to cast off edge.

Knitted Ballet Flats for display only, **pattern not included**

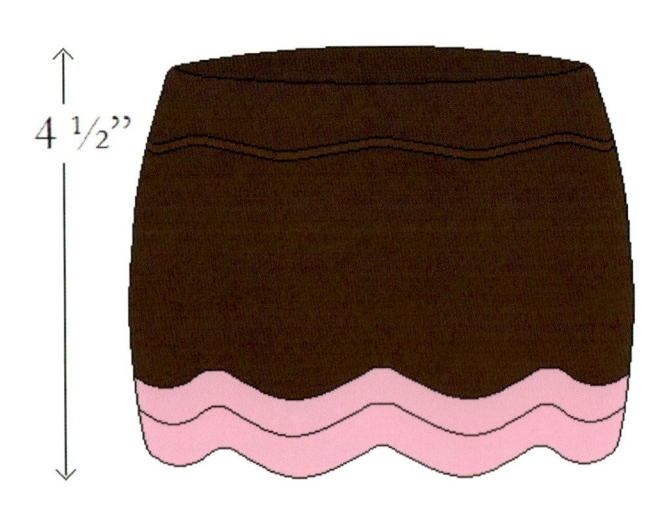

Kimana ~ Neapolitan Chic Collection

Pattern Features: The textured stitch patterns have been written out with line-by-line instructions given, featuring openwork increases resulting in a flattering eyelet pattern on front edges. A shawl collar neckline created from held stitches worked to length and grafted in place. Set in long sleeves with openwork lace pattern.

Construction: Worked flat: Back and forth in rows, from bottom up in one piece to armholes, then each section is worked individually

Materials: 150 – 160 yards (3 – 3 ¼ ounces) of worsted weight yarn, including scraps used for contrast

Knitting Needles: Pair of 3.25mm throughout (US 3-UK/CANADIAN 10)

Notions: Darning Needle, 2 Stitch holders, or Safety Pins

Gauge: Using 3.25mm needles: 6 sts and 7 rows in 1in over chevron stitch

Skill Level: EASY / INTERMEDIATE

Welt:

Begin at lower edge, **cast on 62 sts**, work in **Welt Stitch Pattern**

Welt Stitch Pattern:

Row 1: K across all sts

Row 2: Work in **single ribbing**

These two rows form the pattern stitch

Continue as follows:

Rows 3 – 5: Repeat rows 1 – 2, **one more time**, then work **row 1 only, once more**

Continue onto **Main Body**

by Debonair Designs ~ copyright © 2011 - 2013 Debonair Designs

Kimana ~ Neapolitan Chic Collection

Main Body:

Pattern Note: all slip stitches are slipped knitwise

Right side facing, work in Stitch Pattern

Stitch Pattern:

Row 1: (inc) (K1, P1) two times, sl1, P1, K1, YO, K to last 7 sts; YO, K1, P1, sl1, (K1, P1) two times = *2 sts increased*

Row 2: K4, P (including yarn overs) to last 4 sts; K4

These two rows form the pattern stitch

Continue as follows:

Rows 3 – 14: (inc) Repeat rows 1 – 2, **six more times** = *76 sts*

Continue on to Divide

Divide:

Next Row: (K1, P1) two times, sl1, P1, K1, YO, K10, cast off 8 sts, K until there are 26sts on right-hand needle, cast off 8 sts, K to last 7 sts; YO, K1, P1, sl1, (K1, P1) two times

Continue on to Left Front

Left Front:

Pattern Note: all slip stitches are slipped knitwise

Wrong side facing, work **first 18 sts** in Left Front Stitch Pattern

Left Front Stitch Pattern:

Row 1: K4, P to end

Row 2: (inc) K to last 7 sts; YO, K1, P1, sl1, (K1, P1) two times = *1 st increased*

These two rows form the pattern stitch

Continue as follows:

Rows 3 – 6: (inc) Repeat rows 1 – 2, **two more times** = *21 sts*

Continue on to Neck Shaping

Neck Shaping:

Wrong side facing, work as follows:

Row 1: K4, P to end

Row 2: (dec) K to last 8 sts; K2tog, P1, sl1, (K1, P1) two times = *1 st decreased*

These two rows form the pattern shaping stitch

Continue as follows:

Rows: 3 – 11: (dec) Repeat rows 1 – 2, **four more times**, then work **row 1** *only,* **once more** = *16 sts*

Continue on to Shape Shoulder

Shape Shoulder: Left Front

Next Row: Cast off 9 sts, P1, sl1, (K1, P1) two times, place remaining 7 sts on stitch holder or safety pin

Continue on to Back

Kimana ~ Neapolitan Chic Collection

Back:

Wrong side facing, rejoin yarn to **center 26 sts**, work as follows:

Rows 1 – 15: Beginning with a **purl row**, work in **stockinette stitch**, ending with a purl row

Continue on to Shape Shoulders

Shape Shoulders: Back

Next Row: Cast off 9 sts, K to end

Next Row: Cast off 9 sts, P to end

Cast off remaining sts

Continue on to Right Front

Right Front:

Pattern Note: all slip stitches are slipped knitwise

Wrong side facing, rejoin yarn to **remaining 18 sts**, work in Right Front Stitch Pattern

Right Front Stitch Pattern:

Row 1: P to last 4 sts; K4

Row 2: (inc) (K1, P1) two times, sl1, P1, K1, YO, K to end = *1 st increased*

These two rows form the pattern stitch

Continue as follows:

Rows 3 – 6: (inc) Repeat rows 1 – 2, **two more times** = *21 sts*

Continue on to Neck Shaping

Neck Shaping:

Wrong side facing, work in Shaping Stitch Pattern

Shaping Stitch Pattern:

Row 1: P to last 4 sts; K4

Row 2: (dec) (K1, P1) two times, sl1, P1, ssk, K to end = *1 st decreased*

These two rows form the pattern shaping stitch
Continue as follows:

Rows: 3 – 11: Repeat rows 1 – 2, **four more times**, then work **row 1** *only*, once more = *16 sts*

Continue on to Shape Shoulder

Next Row: (K1, P1) two times, sl1, P1, K1, cast off 9 sts, place remaining 7 sts on stitch holder or safety pin

Right sides together, join shoulder seams

Continue on to Shawl Collar

Kimana ~ Neapolitan Chic Collection

Shawl Collar:

Pattern Note: all slip stitches are slipped knitwise

Right side facing, rejoin yarn to **7 sts held at right front,** work in Shawl Collar Stitch Pattern

Shawl Collar Stitch Pattern:

Row 1: (K1, P1) two times, sl1, P1, K1

Row 2: P3, K4

These two rows form the pattern stitch

Continue as follows:

Rows 3 – 16: Repeat rows 1 – 2, **seven more times**

Cast off all sts loosely

Return next **7sts held at left front** to needle, work as follows:

Row 1: K4, P3

Row 2: K1, P1, sl1, (K1, P1) two times

These two rows form the pattern stitch

Continue as follows:

Rows 3 – 16: Repeat rows 1 – 2, **seven more times**

Cast off all sts loosely

Continue on to Complete Collar

Complete Collar: Right sides together, sew row ends together. Graft lower edge of neckline to cast off edge of main body, align center seam with center of back, weave in yarn break. Fold collar back onto itself, allowing fronts to gently fold for the shawl collar effect.

Continue on to Sleeves

Sleeves: (Both alike)

Sleeve Tip: refer to pg 48

Begin at cuff edge, **cast on 34 sts,** work in Sleeve Stitch Pattern I

Sleeve Stitch Pattern I:

Row 1: (wrong side) K across all sts

Row 2: Work in **single ribbing**

These two rows form the pattern stitch

Rows 3 – 5: Repeat rows 1 – 2, **one more time,** then work **row 1** *only,* once more

Continue on in Lace Stitch Pattern

Lace Stitch Pattern:

(Variation: work rows 1 - 8 in contrast color)

Row 1: P1, K1, P1, * Yrn, P3tog, Yrn, P1, K1, P1, rep from * to last st; K1

Row 2: K2, P1, K1, * P3, K1, P1, K1, rep from * to end

Row 3: P1, K1, P1, * K3, P1, K1, P1, rep from * to last st; K1

Row 4: as row 2

These four rows form the pattern stitch
Continue as follows:

Rows 5 – 8: Repeat rows 1 – 4, **one more time**

(Variation: work row 9 in main color if contrast was used)

Row 9: K across all sts

These nine rows **complete** the lace stitch pattern
Continue as follows:

Kimana ~ Neapolitan Chic Collection Cont

(Variation: continue in main color)

Rows 10 – 14: Repeat rows 1 – 2 of **Sleeve Stitch Pattern I**, (page 60) **two more times**, then work row 1 *only*, **once more**

Rows 15 – 28: Beginning with a **knit row**, work in stockinette stitch

Continue on to Shape Sleeve Top

Shaping Tip: refer to pg 48

Shape Sleeve Top:

Right side facing, work as follows:

Row 1: Cast off 3 sts, K to end

Row 2: Cast off 3 sts, P to end

Row 3: as row 1

Row 4: as row 2

Row 5: as row 1

Row 6: Cast off 3 sts; * P2tog; rep from * to last st; P1 = *9 sts*

Cast off remaining sts

Continue on to Complete

Complete: Right sides together, join sleeve seams to beginning of sleeve top shaping. Wrong side facing, insert to cast off stitches of armhole opening, sew evenly around opening.

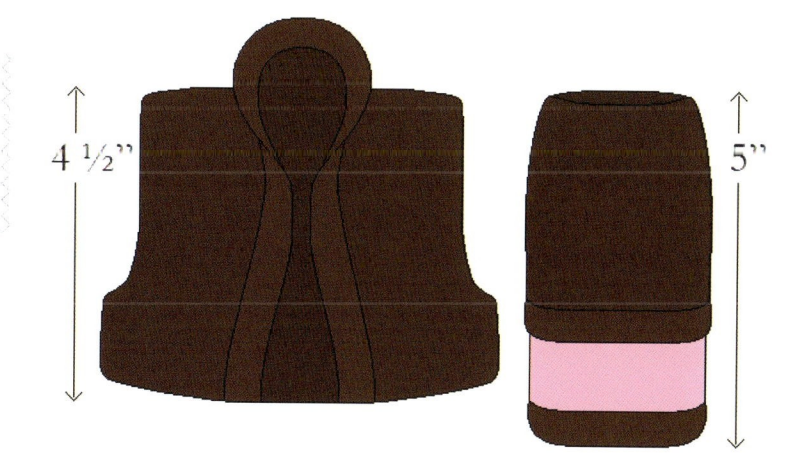

Completed Measurements: approx. 4 ½" from cast on edge to shoulder seam, with a sleeve length of approx. 5" from cuff edge to top of sleeve cap.

Belle ~ Neapolitan Chic Collection

Pattern Features: The textured stitch pattern has been written out with line-by-line instructions given along with variations for working contrast color with optional hat band added at completion

Construction: Worked flat: Back and forth in rows, from brim to shaped crown in one piece with turned up brim, to crown, then seamed

Materials: 65 – 75 yards (1 ¼ - 1 ½ ounces) of worsted weight yarn, including scraps used for contrast

Knitting Needles: Pair of 3.25mm throughout (US 3-UK/CANADIAN 10)

Notion: Darning Needle

Gauge: Using 3.25mm needles: 6 sts and 7 rows in 1in over stockinette stitch

Skill Level:

BEGINNER   EASY

Brim:

Begin at lower edge, **cast on 77 sts,** work as follows:

(Variation: work rows 1 - 7 in contrast color)

Rows 1 – 7: Beginning with a **knit row,** work in **stockinette stitch**

These initial seven rows form the underside of the hat brim

Continue as follows:

Belle ~ Neapolitan Chic Collection Cont

(Variation: row 8, change to main color if contrast was used prior)

Row 8: (wrong side) K across all sts (forms the outer turn ridge)

(Variation: continue in main color)

Rows 9 – 15: Beginning with a **knit row,** work in **stockinette stitch**

These fifteen rows **complete** the brim

Continue on to Crown

Crown:

Row 1: (wrong side) K across all sts

Row 2: (dec) * K5, K2tog, rep from * to end = *66 sts*

Row 3: P across all sts

Continue on in Crown Stitch Pattern

Crown Stitch Pattern:

Row 1: * K4, (P1, K1) three times, P3, rep from * to last st; P1

Row 2: K1, * K3, (P1, K1) three times, P4, rep from * to end

These two rows form the stitch pattern

Continue as follows:

Rows 3 – 16: Repeat rows 1 – 2, **seven more times**

Continue on to Crown Shaping

Crown Shaping:

Row 1: (dec) * K1, K2tog, K1, P1, K1, K2tog, P1, K1, P3, rep from * to last st; P1 = *56 sts*

Row 2: K1, * K3, P1, K1, P2, K1, P3, rep from * to end

Row 3: * K3, P1, K2, P1, K1, P3, rep from * to last st; P1

Row 4: as row 2

Row 5: (dec) * K1, K2tog, P1, K2, P1, K1, P2tog, P1, rep from * to last st; P1 = *46 sts*

Belle ~ **Neapolitan Chic Collection** Cont

Row 6: K1, * K2, P1, K1, P2, K1, P2, rep from * to end

Row 7: (dec) * K2tog, P1, K2tog, P1, K1, P2, rep from * to last st; P1 = *36 sts*

Row 8: K1, * K2, P1, (K1, P1) two times, rep from * to end

Row 9: (dec) * (K1, P1) two times, K1, P2tog, rep from * to last st; P1 = *31 sts*

Row 10: K1, * K1, P1, rep from * to end

Row 11: (dec) K1, * P1, K3tog, rep from * to last 2 sts; P2 = *17 sts*

Row 12: (dec) * K2tog, rep from * to last st; P1 = *9 sts*

Continue on to **Complete Hat**

Complete Hat: Break yarn and thread through remaining stitches, drawing up firmly and fasten securely. Join seam. **Completed Measurements:** Designed to fit head circumference of 13" (33cm) approx.

Hat Band:

Cast on 180 sts, work as follows:

Row 1: K across all sts

Rows 2 – 3: Work in **single ribbing**

Cast off loosely

Continue on to **Complete**

Complete Hat Band: Weave in yarn breaks, tie loosely around hat brim forming a bow, secure bow center. **Completed Measurements:** Designed to fit head circumference of 13" (33cm) approx.

BoHoh II ~ Neapolitan Chic Collection

Pattern Features: The textured stitch pattern has been written out with line-by-line instructions given along with variations for working contrast color

Construction: Worked flat: Back and forth in rows, in one piece with fold down button flap then seamed, strap added at completion

Materials: 33 – 35 yards (1 ounce) of MEDIUM 4 worsted weight yarn, including scraps used for contrast

Knitting Needles: Pair of 3.25mm throughout (US 3-UK/CANADIAN 10)

Notions: 1 Button (size optional) used for flap closure, Crochet Hook (size F) used for strap (optional), Darning Needle

Gauge: Using 3.25mm needles: 6 sts and 7 rows in 1in over stockinette stitch

Skill Level: BEGINNER   EASY

Stitch Pattern

Row 1: (right side) P4, (K1, P1) four times, K6, (P1, K1) four times, P4

Row 2: K4, (P1, K1) four times, P6, (K1, P1) four times, K4

These two rows form the pattern stitch

Rows: 3 – 10: Repeat rows 1 – 2, **four more times**

(Variation: work rows 11 – 12 in contrast color)

Rows 11 – 12: Work in **garter stitch**

Rows 13 – 20: Repeat rows 1 – 2, **four more times**

(Variation: work rows 21 – 22 in contrast color)

Rows 21 – 22: Work in **garter stitch**

Rows 23 – 24: Repeat rows 1 – 2, **one more time**

Main Piece:

The following rows form the front, begin at top edge, **cast on 22 sts,** work as follows:
(Variation: work in contrast color)

Row 1: K across all sts

Row 2: (inc) K4, kfb in next 4 sts, P6, kfb in next 4 sts, K4 = *30 sts*

Continue and work in Stitch Pattern

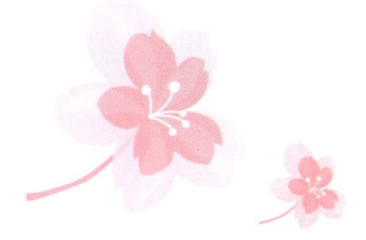

BoHoh II ~ Neapolitan Chic Collection Cont

The following rows form the base

(Variation: work rows 25 – 26 in contrast color)

Rows 25 – 26: Work in **garter stitch**

Row 27: P across all sts

Row 28: (wrong side) K across all sts (forms bottom turn ridge)

The following rows form the back

Rows 29 – 30: Repeat rows 1 – 2, **one more time**

(Variation: work rows 31 – 32 in contrast color)

Rows 31 – 32: Work in **garter stitch**

Rows 33 – 40: Repeat rows 1 – 2, **four more times**

(Variation: work rows 41 – 42 in contrast color)

Rows 41 – 42: Work in **garter stitch**

Rows: 43 – 52: Repeat rows 1 – 2, **five more times**

Continue on to Flap

Flap:

Work as follows: (Variation: work in contrast color)

Row 1: (dec) P2tog, P2, (K1, P1) four times, (P2tog) three times, (P1, K1) four times, P2, P2tog = *25 sts*

Row 2: (wrong side) K across all sts

Row 3: (dec) P2tog, P1, (K1, P1) four times, P3, (P1, K1) four times, P1, P2tog = *23 sts*

Row 4: as row 2

Row 5: (dec) P2tog, (K1, P1) four times, P2tog, P1, (P1, K1) four times, P2tog = *20 sts*

Row 6: as row 2

Row 7: * P1, K1, rep from * to end

Row 8: as row 2

Row 9: (dec) P2tog, (K1, P1) eight times, P2tog = *18 sts*

Row 10: (buttonhole) K8, YO, K2tog, K8

(* Variation: work 2 buttonholes for ribbon tie fastener)

* Row 10: (2 buttonholes) K6, YO, K2tog, K2, YO, K2tog, K6

Row 11: as row 7

Row 12: as row 2

Cast off all sts knitwise, continue on to Complete

Complete: Right sides together, fold cast on edge up to beginning of flap, sew row ends together. Turn right side out, fold flap down, sew on button. Variation: attach two ribbon lengths to front, thread through two buttonholes, tie in bow to fasten. **Strap:** Work a crochet chain stitch to desired length. **Tip:** refer to pg 48. Attach length to purl sts on one side starting at bottom, leave a loop for shoulder strap, attach to other side.

From The Sea

From the Sea Collection ~
Abbreviations & Tips

Standard Abbreviations:

Refer to pg viii

Stitch Patterns:

Stockinette Stitch = knit a row, purl a row

Garter Stitch = knit every row

Seed Stitch = knit 1, purl 1, knit 1 every row

Crocheted Chain Stitch:
as pictured →

Tip for Sleeves/Legs: Cast on stitches for each sleeve/leg on the same needle, using separate skeins for each one, and working them at the same time

Tip for Sleeve Top Shaping: When working the cast off stitches over several rows as indicated, slip the first of the cast off stitches, then proceed with cast off, this makes for a smoother transition

Pattern Tip: For working the contrast stripe pattern, I like to make use of two skeins, one for each end of the main color, with a third skein of the contrast, thus eliminating extra yarn breaks, be sure to wrap the contrast with the main color to avoid gaps in color work

Pattern Note: Worked flat: Back and forth in rows

Construction: Refer to individual pattern pages for details

Skill Level: Refer to individual pattern pages for details

Materials: Refer to individual pattern pages for quantities

4 MEDIUM Worsted/10ply yarn used throughout

Yarn Equivalent: 8 ply, Aran (UK)

Twisted Cord: ↓

1. Making a twisted cord requires several strands of yarn each about 2 – 3 times the required length and even, cut the strands and knot together at each end.

2. Attach one end to a pin, or door handle, insert a knitting needle through the other end, twist the needle anticlockwise until the strands are well twisted together, the tighter the strands are twisted, the firmer the finished cord will be, this will also reduce the finished length.

3. Holding the center of the cord, place the needle end and the hook end together, keeping the cord taut to avoid tangling. Release the center of the cord and allow the two halves to twist together smoothing out the bumps. Knot and trim both ends.

SEASONAL HAND KNITTED DESIGNS FOR 18" DOLLS ~ SPRING/SUMMER COLLECTION

FROM THE SEA COLLECTION

~ 4

From the Sea Collection

When designing this nautical collection, the featured chevron stitch pattern found in Adrift reminded me of the gentle ripples of a flowing tide along with waves cresting upon a rocky shoreline. With the addition of trendy pieces, nautical fashion is still considered today as timeless symbols of escape to distant shores. A versatile addition for your doll's transitional wardrobe.

~ Debonair Designs

Model wearing **Adrift** paired with **Kiah Jumpsuit** and **Eyelet Beret**

From the Sea Collection Patterns:

Adrift ~ a chevron stitched cardigan . . . . . . .Pg 70

Kiah ~ a lace stitched jumpsuit
or bib top playsuit . . . . Pg 75

Charter ~ a textured stitched hooded jacket . Pg 84

Eyelet Beret ~ a stylish eyelet beret. . . . . . . .Pg 91

Model wearing **Charter** paired with **Kiah Playsuit**

- 69 -

by Debonair Designs ~ copyright © 2011 - 2013 Debonair Designs

SEASONAL HAND KNITTED DESIGNS FOR 18" DOLLS ~ SPRING/SUMMER COLLECTION

Adrift ~ From the Sea Collection

Pattern Features: The chevron stitch pattern has been written out with line-by-line instructions given, along with buttonhole placement and variations. A classic crew neckline created from picked up stitches and set in sleeves that have a slight bell shape on the bottom.

Construction: Worked flat: Back and forth in rows, from bottom up in one piece to armholes, then each section worked individually.

Materials: 90 – 120 yards (2 – 2 ½ ounces) of worsted weight yarn

Knitting Needles: Pair of 3.25mm throughout (US 3-UK/CANADIAN 10)

Notions: 3 Buttons size 9/16" (13mm), Darning Needle, 2 Stitch Holders or Safety Pins

Gauge: Using 3.25mm needles: 7 sts and 6 rows in 1in over stockinette stitch

Skill Level: EASY — INTERMEDIATE

Model wearing Adrift worked using four stripe variation, paired with Kiah and Eyelet Beret

Main Body: (Includes 3 sts worked in garter stitch at each end for button bands indicated in *italics*)

Pattern Note: for working **stripe pattern** follow main body with variation indicated *

Begin at lower edge and main color, **cast on 78 sts**, work as follows:

Rows 1 – 2: Work in **garter stitch**

Continue on in Stitch Pattern

Model wearing Adrift worked using three stripe variation →

- 70 -

by Debonair Designs ~ copyright © 2011 - 2013 Debonair Designs

Adrift ~ From the Sea Collection Cont

Stitch Pattern:

Row 1: (1st buttonhole) *K1, YO, K2tog,* ***** YO, K2, K2tog, K2, rep from ***** to last 3 sts; *K3*

Row 2: *K3,* P (including yarn overs) to last 3 sts, *K3*

Row 3: *K3,* ***** K2, K2tog, K2, YO, rep from ***** to last 3 sts; *K3*

Row 4: as row 2

These four rows form the pattern stitch

Continue on to <u>next rows in order</u> ↓ for a plain cardigan or follow ***** for **Stripe Pattern** next column →

Rows 5 – 16: Repeat rows 1 – 4, **three more times** omit buttonhole, work garter stitch as established

Rows 17 – 20: Repeat rows 1 – 4, **one more time,** work buttonhole as indicated on row 1, thus working a 2nd buttonhole

Rows 21 – 22: Work in **garter stitch**

Continue on to Divide

* (Variation: For **Stripe Pattern,** work rows <u>5 – 16</u> in following manner ↓)

Pattern Note: When working the contrast for pattern stripe on row 5, K3 in main color, the YO will be in contrast color.
Pattern Tip: for working contrast, refer to pg 68

Row 5: *Using main color, K3,* join on contrast, ***** YO, K2, K2tog, K2, rep from ***** to last 3 sts; *using main color, K3*

Row 6: *Using main color, K3,* with contrast P (including yarn overs) to last 3 sts, *using main color, K3*

Rows 7 – 8: *Using main color,* repeat rows 3 – 4, **once more**

Rows 9 – 10: Repeat rows 5 – 6, **once more**

Rows 11 – 12: *Using main color,* repeat rows 3 – 4, **once more**

Rows 13 – 14: Repeat rows 5 – 6, **once more**

Rows 15 – 16: *Using main color,* repeat rows 3 – 4, **once more**

(Variation: break contrast, continue in main color or <u>work a fourth stripe</u> as established above)

Rows 17 – 20: Repeat rows 1 – 4, **one more time,** work buttonhole as indicated on row 1, thus working a 2nd buttonhole

Rows 21 – 22: Work in **garter stitch**

Continue on to Divide

Divide:

Next Row: K17, cast off 8 sts, K until 28 sts are on right hand needle, cast off 8 sts, K to end

Continue on to Left Front

Adrift ~ From the Sea Collection

Left Front: (Includes 3 sts worked in garter stitch for button band indicated in *italics*)

Work on **first 17 sts** in Left Front Stitch Pattern

Left Front Stitch Pattern:

Row 1: (wrong side) *K3*, P to end

Row 2: K to last 3 sts; *K3*

These two rows form the pattern stitch

Continue as follows:

Rows 3 – 12: Repeat rows 1 – 2, **five more times**

Continue on to Neck Shaping

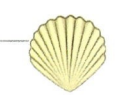

Neck Shaping:

Row 1: (wrong side) *K3*, place on hold, sl1 *purlwise*, P1, PSSO, P to end

Row 2: K to last 2 sts; K2tog tbl

Row 3: S1, P1, PSSO, P to end

Row 4: as row 2

Rows 5 – 6: Repeat rows 3 – 4, **once more** = *8 sts*

Cast off remaining 8 sts for shoulder, continue on to Back

Back:

Wrong side facing and main color, rejoin yarn to **center 28 sts,** work as follows:

Rows 1 – 19: Beginning with a **purl row,** work in **stockinette stitch**

(Variation: work a contrast color every two rows for stripe pattern as established for front)

Continue on to Shape Shoulders

Shape Shoulders:

Next Row: Cast off 8 sts, K to end.

Next Row: Cast off 8 sts, P to end.

Cast off remaining 12 sts

Continue on to Right Front

Right Front: (Includes 3 sts worked in garter stitch for button band indicated in *italics*)

Wrong side facing, rejoin yarn to **remaining 17 sts,** work in Right Front Stitch Pattern

Right Front Stitch Pattern:

Row 1: (wrong side) P to last 3 sts; *K3*

Row 2: *K3*, K to end

These two rows form the pattern stitch

Continue as follows:

Rows 3 – 7: Repeat rows 1 – 2, **two more times,** then work **row 1** *only*, **once more**

Row 8: (3rd buttonhole) K1, YO, K2tog, K to end

Rows 9 – 11: Repeat rows 1 – 2, **one more time,** then work **row 1** *only,* **once more**

Continue on to Neck Shaping

Adrift ~ From the Sea Collection Cont

Neck Shaping:

Row 1: (right side) *K3,* place on hold, * sl1, K1, PSSO, K to end

Row 2: P to last 2 sts; P2tog

Rows 3 – 6: Repeat rows 1 – 2, **two more times** = *8 sts*

Row 7: K across all sts.

Cast off remaining 8 sts for shoulder

Right sides together, join shoulder seams

Continue on to Crew Neckline

Crew Neckline: (Includes 3 sts worked in garter stitch for button bands indicated in *italics*)

Right side facing, rejoin main color to the 3 sts held, K3, pick up and K11 sts evenly up right front, (including across shoulder seam), 14 sts across back, 11 sts down left front (including across shoulder seam) 3 sts held = *42 sts*

Continue on to Crew Neckline Stitch Pattern

Crew Neckline Stitch Pattern:

Row 1: (wrong side) *K3,* * P1, K1, rep from * to last 3 sts; *K3*

Rows 2 – 3: Repeat row 1, **two more times**

Cast off in pattern

Continue on to Sleeves

Sleeves: Both alike

Sleeve Tip: refer to pg 68

Begin at cuff edge, **cast on 38 sts,** work as follows:

Rows 1 – 2: Work in **garter stitch**

Continue on in Sleeve Stitch Pattern

Sleeve Stitch Pattern:

Row 1: (right side) K1, * YO, K2, K2tog, K2, rep from * to last st; K1

Row 2: P (including yarn overs) across all sts

Row 3: K1, * K2, K2tog, K2, YO, rep from * to last st; K1

Row 4: as row 2

These four rows form the pattern stitch

Pattern Note: for working **stripe pattern** follow variation indicated *

* (Variation: work a contrast color on rows 1- 2 *only* of each pattern repeat , thereby working three stripes)

Rows 5 – 16: Repeat rows 1 – 4, **three more times**

* (Variation: break contrast and continue in main color or work a fourth stripe as established above)

Rows 17 – 20: Repeat Rows 1 – 2, **one more time**

Row 21: (dec) * K2tog tbl, K16, rep from * to last 2sts; K2tog tbl = *35 sts*

Row 22: P across all sts

Rows 23 – 24: Work in **garter stitch**

Rows 25 – 30: Beginning with a **knit row,** work in **stockinette stitch**

Continue on to Shape Sleeve Top

Adrift ~ From the Sea Collection Cont

Shaping Tip: refer to pg 68

Shape Sleeve Top:

Right side facing, work as follows:

Row 1: Cast off 3 sts, K to end

Row 2: Cast off 3 sts, P to end

Row 3: as row 1

Row 4: as row 2

Row 5: as row 1

Row 6: Cast off 3 sts, * P2tog; rep from * to end = *6 sts*

Cast off these remaining sts

Continue on to Complete

Complete: Right sides together, join sleeve seams to beginning of sleeve top shaping. Wrong side facing, insert to cast off stitches of armhole opening, sew evenly around opening. Sew on buttons.

Model wearing **Adrift** worked with four stripes, see variation

Completed Measurement: approx. 6" from cast on edge to shoulder seam, with a sleeve length of approx. 5" from cuff edge to top of sleeve cap.

by Debonair Designs ~ copyright © 2011 - 2013 Debonair Designs

Kiah ~ From the Sea Collection

*Models wearing **Kiah** lace top long version at left with bib top shorter version at right*

Pattern Features: The stitch pattern has been written out with line-by-line instructions given including back-buttonhole placement, a lace stitched bodice worked for the jumpsuit or a bib top worked for the playsuit along with a long or short version.

Construction: Worked flat: Back and forth in rows. Each leg section is worked separately from the cuff up, then joined and worked in one piece to armholes, then each section is worked individually.

Materials: 200 – 230 yards (4 – 4 ½ ounces) of worsted weight yarn, including scraps used for contrast

Knitting Needles: Pair of 3.25mm throughout (US 3-UK/CANADIAN 10)

Notions: 3 Buttons size ½" (12mm), 2 extra Buttons needed for bib top version worked at completion, Darning Needle

Gauge: Using 3.25mm needles: 5 sts and 7 rows in 1in over stockinette stitch

Skill Level: EASY   INTERMEDIATE

Legs: Both alike

Pattern Note: Both long and short version are worked the same, short version work until * has been reached. The lace bodice jumpsuit and bib top playsuit are worked the same until ** has been reached
Leg Tip: refer to pg 68

Begin at cuff edge of leg, **cast on 45sts** work as follows:

(Variation: cast on and work set up row in contrast color)

Set up Row: K across all sts

Continue on in Cuff Stitch Pattern

- 75 -

by Debonair Designs ~ copyright © 2011 - 2013 Debonair Designs

Kiah Jumpsuit/Playsuit ~ From the Sea Collection Cont

Cuff Stitch Pattern:

(Variation: work rows 1 – 10 in contrast color)

Row 1: * (K2tog *knitwise*, YF) two times, K1, (YF, K2tog tbl) two times; repeat from * to end

Row 2: P (including made stitches from yf) across all sts

These two rows form the pattern stitch

Continue as follows:

Rows 3 – 8: Repeat rows 1 – 2, **three more times**

(Variation: work rows 9 – 10 in contrast if main color was used for stitch pattern)

Rows 9 – 10: K across all sts

These ten rows **complete** the pattern stitch

* Continue on to select length:

* For short version work as follows:

Rows 11 – 14: Beginning with a **knit row,** work in **stockinette stitch**

(Mark each end of last row to be used at completion)

Continue on to Shape Body

For long version work as follows:

Rows 11 – 22: Beginning with a **knit row,** work in **stockinette stitch** (Variation: Increase length further here by working more rows until desired length, ending with purl row)

(Mark each end of last row to be used at completion.)

Continue on to Shape Body

Shape Body: (both long & short versions)

Row 1: (dec) K2tog, K to end

Row 2: (dec) P2tog, P to end

Rows 3 – 6: (dec) Repeat rows 1 – 2, **two more times** = *39sts*

Rows 7 – 18: Beginning with a **knit row,** work in **stockinette stitch**

Place sts on hold, work second leg in same manner

Continue on to Join legs for Upper Body

Join legs for Upper Body:

Next Row: (dec right side facing) work sts held for one leg as follows: K14, (K2tog) three times, K17, slip 1, K1, PSSO, using same needle work sts held for second leg as follows: slip 1, K1, PSSO, K17, (K2tog) three times, K to end = *70 sts*

Next Row: (dec) K1, P1, K1, P31, P2tog, P to last 3 sts; K1, P1, K1 = *69 sts* **

** For Jumpsuit continue on to Lace Bodice pg 77

** For Playsuit continue on to Bib Top pg 80

Kiah Jumpsuit ~ From the Sea Collection

Lace Bodice: (Includes 3 sts worked in seed stitch at each end for button bands indicated in *italics*)

Work in Lace Stitch Pattern

Lace Stitch Pattern:

Row 1: *K1, P1, K1,* K18, [(K2tog *knitwise*, YF) two times, K1, (YF, K2tog tbl) two times] three times, K to last 3 sts; *K1, P1, K1*

Row 2: *K1, P1, K1,* P to last 3 sts; (including made stitches from yf), *K1, P1, K1*

These two rows form the pattern stitch
Continue as follows:

Rows 3 – 18: Repeat rows 1 – 2, **eight more times**

Continue on to Divide

Divide:

Next Row: *K1, P1, K1,* K11, cast off 7 sts, K1, YF, K2tog *knitwise*, YF, K1, (YF, K2tog tbl) two times, [(K2tog *knitwise*, YF) two times, K1, (YF, K2tog tbl) two times] two times, cast off 7 sts, K to last 3 sts; *K1, P1, K1*

Continue on to Right Back

Right Back: (Includes 3 sts worked in seed stitch for button band indicated in *italics*)

Wrong side facing, work on **last 14 sts** in Right Back Stitch Pattern

Right Back Stitch Pattern:

Row 1: *K1, P1, K1,* P to last 2 sts; K2

Row 2: K to last 3 sts; *K1, P1, K1*

These two rows form the pattern stitch
Continue as follows:

Model wearing **Lace Top Kiah** long version, sleeveless **Charter** pictured in background

Rows: 3 – 17: Repeat rows 1 – 2, **seven more times,** then work **row 1** *only,* **once more**

Continue on to Shape Shoulder

Shape Shoulder:

Next Row: Cast off 8sts, K to last 3 sts; *K1, P1, K1*

Next Row: *K1, P1, K1,* P to end

Cast off remaining 6 sts, continue on to Lace Bodice Front

Kiah Jumpsuit ~ From the Sea Collection

Lace Bodice Front:

Wrong side facing, rejoin yarn to **center 28 sts** work in Front Stitch Pattern

Front Stitch Pattern:

Row 1: P across all sts

Row 2: K1, * (K2tog *knitwise*, YF) two times, K1, (YF, K2tog tbl) two times; repeat from * to end

These two rows form the pattern stitch

Continue as follows:

Rows 3 – 7: Repeat rows 1 – 2, **two more times**, then work **row 1** *only*, **once more**

Continue on to Neck Shaping

Neck Shaping :

Right side facing, work as follows:

Row 1: K1, (K2tog *knitwise*, YF) two times, K1, (YF, K2tog tbl) two times, K2tog *knitwise*, YF, K2tog *knitwise, turn*

Row 2: P2tog, P to end

Row 3: K1, (K2tog *knitwise*, YF) two times, K1, (YF, K2tog tbl) two times, K2tog *knitwise, turn*

Row 4: as row 2

Row 5: K1, (K2tog *knitwise*, YF) two times, K1, YF K2tog tbl, YF, K2tog *knitwise, turn*

Row 6: as row 2

Row 7: K1, (K2tog *knitwise*, YF) two times, K1, YF, K2tog tbl, K1, *turn*

Row 8: as row 2 *= 8 sts*

Row 9: K1, (K2tog *knitwise*, YF) two times, K1, YF, K2tog tbl, *turn*

Row 10: Purl across all sts

Row 11: as row 9

Row 12: as row 10

Cast off remaining 8 sts for shoulder

Right side facing, rejoin to left side stitches, work as follows:

Row 1: K1, (YF, K2tog tbl) two times, (K2tog *knitwise*, YF) two times, K1, (YF, K2tog tbl) two times

Row 2: P to last 2 sts; P2tog

Row 3: K2tog *knitwise*, YF, K2tog tbl, (K2tog *knitwise*, YF*)* two times, K1, (YF, K2tog tbl) two times

Row 4: as row 2

Row 5: K2tog *knitwise*, (K2tog *knitwise*, YF) two times, K1, (YF, K2tog tbl) two times

Row 6: as row 2

Row 7: (K2tog *knitwise*, YF*)* two times, K1, (YF, K2tog tbl) two times

Row 8: as row 2 *= 8 sts*

Row 9: K1, K2tog *knitwise*, YF, K1, (YF, K2tog tbl) two times

Row 10: Purl across all sts

Row 11: as row 9

Row 12: as row 10

Cast off remaining 8 sts for shoulder, continue on to Left Back

Kiah Jumpsuit ~ From the Sea Collection

Left Back: (Includes 3 sts worked in seed stitch for button band indicated in *italics*)

Wrong side facing, rejoin yarn to **remaining 14 sts** in Left Back Stitch Pattern

Left Back Stitch Pattern:

Row 1: K2, P to last 3 sts; *K1, P1, K1*

Row 2: *K1, P1, K1,* K to end

These two rows form the pattern stitch

Continue as follows:

Rows 3 – 16: Repeat rows 1 – 2, **seven more times**

Continue on to Shape Shoulder

Shape Shoulder:

Next Row: Cast off 8sts, P to last 3 sts; *K1, P1, K1*

Next Row: *K1, P1, K1,* K to end

Cast off remaining 6 sts

Continue on to Complete

Complete: Right sides together, match up row ends, sew from beginning of button bands at back down to marker and at beginning of waist down to marker, these seams will become center seams of front and back, match these seams together and continue to sew rows ends of legs together to cast on edge, creating inside leg seams. Right sides together, sew shoulder seams. Using a crochet hook, chain stitch approx 10 sts for button loops. **Tip:** refer to pg 68, attach to button bands at back and sew on buttons. **Optional Decoration:** Work a length of twisted cord **Tip:** refer to pg 68, add at front section just under the lace bodice, secure at each end with decorative buttons and form into a bow (as pictured).

Completed Jumpsuit Measurements: approx. 10 ¾" from leg cuff edge to shoulder seam. Shorter version: approx. 9 ¾" from leg cuff edge to shoulder seam.

Kiah Playsuit~ From the Sea Collection

Bib Top: (Includes 3 sts worked in seed stitch at each end for button bands indicated in *italics*)

Continue and work in Bib Stitch Pattern

Bib Stitch Pattern:

Row 1: *K1, P1, K1,* K to last 3 sts; *K1, P1, K1*

Row 2: *K1, P1, K1,* P to last 3 sts; *K1, P1, K1*

These two rows form the pattern stitch

Continue as follows:

Rows 3 – 14: Repeat rows 1 – 2, **six more times**

Continue on to Bib Stitch Pattern II

Bib Stitch Pattern II:

Row 1: *K1, P1, K1,* K23, (P1, K1) eight times, P1, K to last 3 sts; *K1, P1, K1*

Row 2: *K1, P1, K1,* P24, (K1, P1) eight times, P to last 3 sts; *K1, P1, K1*

These two rows form the pattern stitch

Continue as follows:

Rows 3 – 4: Repeat rows 1 – 2, **one more time**

Continue on to Divide

Divide:

Next Row: *K1, P1, K1,* K11, cast off 7 sts, K4, P1, K1, P1, K11, P1, K1, P1, K5, cast off 7 sts, K to last 3 sts; *K1, P1, K1*

Continue on to Right Back

Right Back: (Includes 3 sts worked in seed stitch for button band indicated in *italics*)

Wrong side facing, work on **last 14 sts** in Right Back Stitch Pattern

Right Back Stitch Pattern:

Row 1: *K1, P1, K1,* P to last 3 sts; K1, P1, K1

Row 2: K1, P1, K to last 3 sts; *K1, P1, K1*

These two rows form the pattern stitch

Continue as follows:

Rows: 3 – 12: Repeat rows 1 – 2, **five more times**

Continue on to Neckline and Strap

*Model wearing **Bib Top Kiah** short version, paired with sleeveless version of **Charter***

Kiah Playsuit ~ From the Sea Collection

Neckline and Strap:

Wrong side facing, work as follows:

Next Row: Cast off 6 sts, P4, K1, P1, K1

Continue on to Strap Stitch Pattern

Strap Stitch Pattern:

Row 1: K1, P1, K4, P1, K1

Row 2: K1, P1, K1, P2, K1, P1, K1

These two rows form the pattern stitch

Continue as follows:

Rows 3 – 22: Repeat rows 1 – 2, **ten more times**

Row 23: (buttonhole) K1, P1, K1, YO, K2tog, K1, P1, K1

Row 24: as row 2

Row 25: as row 1

Cast off remaining 8 sts, continue on to Bib Top Front

Bib Top Front:

Wrong side facing, rejoin yarn to **center 27 sts** work in Front Stitch Pattern

Front Stitch Pattern:

Row 1: K2, P4, K1, P13, K1, P4, K2

Row 2: K5, P1, K1, P1, K11, P1, K1, P1, K5

These two rows form the pattern stitch

Continue as follows:

Model wearing **Bib Top Kiah** short version

Rows 3 – 8: Repeat rows 1 – 2, **three more times**

Row 9: K2, P4, (K1, P1) seven times, K1, P4, K2

Row 10: K5, (P1, K1) eight times, P1, K5

Row 11: as row 1

Continue on to Neckline and Strap

Kiah Playsuit ~ From the Sea Collection Cont

Neckline and Strap:

Row 1: K5, P1, K1, P1 *turn*

Row 2: P1, K1, P4, K2

These two rows form the pattern stitch

Continue as follows:

Rows 3 – 4: Repeat rows 1 – 2, **one more time**

Cast off remaining 8 sts, break yarn and rejoin to remaining 19 sts, work as follows:

Row 1: Cast off 11 sts, K1, P1, K5

Row 2: K2, P4, K1, P1

Row 3: P1, K1, P1, K5

Row 4: as row 2

Cast off remaining 8 sts, continue on to Left Back

Left Back: (Includes 3 sts worked in seed stitch for button band indicated in *italics*)

Wrong side facing, rejoin yarn to **remaining 14 sts** in Left Back Stitch Pattern

Left Back Stitch Pattern:

Row 1: K1, P1, K1, P to last 3 sts; *K1, P1, K1*

Row 2: *K1, P1, K1,* K to last 2 sts; P1, K1

These two rows form the pattern stitch

Continue as follows:

Rows 3 – 13: Repeat rows 1 – 2, **five more times,** then work **row 1** *only,* **once more**

Continue on to Neckline and Strap

Neckline and Strap:

Right side facing, work as follows:

Next Row: Cast off 6 sts, K4, K1, P1, K1

Continue on to Strap Stitch Pattern

Strap Stitch Pattern:

Row 1: K1, P1, K1, P2, K1, P1, K1

Row 2: K1, P1, K4, P1, K1

These two rows form the pattern stitch
Continue as follows:

Rows 3 – 21: Repeat rows 1 – 2, **nine more times,** then work **row 1** *only,* **once more**

Row 22: (buttonhole) K1, P1, K1, YO, K2tog, K1, P1, K1

Rows 23 – 24: Repeat rows 1 – 2, **one more time**

Cast off remaining 8 sts

Continue on to Complete

Kiah Playsuit ~ From the Sea Collection Cont

Complete: Right sides together, match up row ends, sew from beginning of button bands at back down to marker and at beginning of waist down to marker, these seams will become center seams of front and back, match these seams together and continue to sew rows ends of legs together to cast on edge, creating inside leg seams. Using a crochet hook, chain stitch approx 10 sts for button loops. **Tip:** refer to pg 68, attach to button bands at back and sew on buttons. Sew buttons on front bib top tabs to align with buttonholes on straps.

Completed Playsuit Measurements: approx. 10 ¾" from leg cuff edge to top of shoulder. **Shorter version:** approx. 9 ¾" from leg cuff edge to top of shoulder.

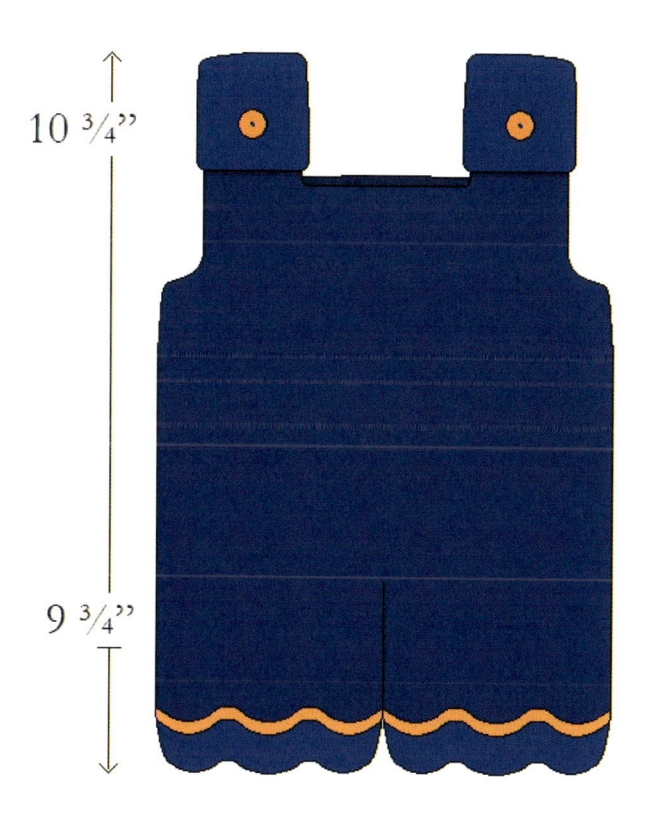

Models wearing **Kiah** lace top and bib top version

SEASONAL HAND KNITTED DESIGNS FOR 18" DOLLS ~ SPRING/SUMMER COLLECTION

Charter ~ From the Sea Collection

Pattern Features: The textured ribbed stitch pattern has been written out with line-by-line instructions given, along with buttonhole placement and variations. A trendy paneled hood along with a sleeveless option.

Construction: Worked flat: Back and forth in rows, from bottom up in one piece to armholes, then each section worked individually.

Materials: 230 – 250 yards (4 ½ - 5 ounces) of worsted weight yarn

Knitting Needles: Pair of 3.75mm throughout (US 5-UK/CANADIAN 9)

Notions: 4 Buttons size ½" (12mm), Darning Needle

Gauge: Using 3.75mm needles: 6 sts and 7 rows in 1in over stockinette stitch

Skill Level: EASY   INTERMEDIATE

*Model wearing **Charter** sleeveless version, paired with **Kiah***

Welt:

Begin at lower edge, **cast on 76 sts,** work as follows:

Rows 1 – 2: Work in **garter stitch**

Rows 3 – 4: Work in **single ribbing**

Rows 5 – 6: Work in **garter stitch**

These six rows **complete** the welt

Continue on to Main Body

- 84 -

by Debonair Designs ~ copyright © 2011 - 2013 Debonair Designs

Charter ~ From the Sea Collection

Main Body: (Includes 3 sts worked in seed stitch at each end for button bands indicated in *italics*)

Right side facing, work in Stitch Pattern

Stitch Pattern:

Row 1: (1st buttonhole) *K1, YO, K2tog,* K5, (P1, K1) three times, P5, K10, (P1, K1) three times, P6, (K1, P1) three times, K10, P5, (K1, P1) three times, K5, *K1, P1, K1*

Row 2: *K1, P1, K1,* P5, (K1, P1) three times, K1, P2, K2, P10, (K1, P1) three times, K6, (P1, K1) three times, P10, K2, P2, K1, (P1, K1) three times, P5, *K1, P1, K1*

Rows 3 – 4: Repeat rows 1 – 2, **one more time,** omit buttonhole, work seed stitch as established

Row 5: *K1, P1, K1,* K5, (P1, K1) three times, P15, (P1, K1) three times, P6, (K1, P1) three times, P15, (K1, P1) three times, K5, *K1, P1, K1*

Row 6: as row 2

Rows 7 – 9: Repeat rows 1 – 2, **one more time,** then work **row 1** *only,* **once more,** omit buttonhole, work seed stitch as established

Row 10: *K1, P1, K1,* P5, (K1, P1) three times, K1, P2, K12, (K1, P1) three times, K6, (P1, K1) three times, K12, P2, K1, (P1, K1) three times, P5, *K1, P1, K1*

These ten rows form the pattern stitch

Continue as follows:

Model wearing **Charter** paired with **Kiah**

Rows 11 – 20: Repeat rows 1 – 10, **one more time,** work buttonhole as indicated on row 1, thus working a 2nd buttonhole

Rows 21 – 24: Repeat rows 1 – 4, **once more,** work buttonhole as indicated on row 1, thus working a 3rd buttonhole

Continue on to Divide

Divide:

Next Row: *K1, P1, K1,* K5, (P1, K1) three times, P3, cast off 8 sts, P3, (P1, K1) three times, P6, (K1, P1) three times, P4, cast off 8 sts, P2, (K1, P1) three times, K5, *K1, P1, K1*

Continue on to Left Front

- 85 -

Charter ~ From the Sea Collection

Left Front: (Includes 3 sts worked in seed stitch for button band indicated in *italics*)

Wrong side facing, work **first 17 sts** in Left Front Stitch Pattern

Left Front Stitch Pattern:

Row 1: *K1, P1, K1,* P5, (K1, P1,) three times, K1, P2

Row 2: P3, (K1, P1,) three times, K5, *K1, P1, K1*

These two rows form the pattern stitch
Continue as follows:

Rows 3 – 17: Repeat rows 1 – 2, **seven more times,** then work **row 1** *only,* once more

Continue on to Shape Shoulder

Shape Shoulder:

Next Row: Cast off 8 sts, K5, *K1, P1, K1*

Next Row: *K1, P1, K1,* P6

Continue on to Left Hood Panel Shaping

Left Hood Panel Shaping: (Includes 3 sts worked in seed stitch for band edging indicated in *italics*)

Right side facing, continue as follows:

Row 1: (inc) K1, kfb in next 4 sts, K1, *K1, P1, K1* = *13 sts*

Row 2: *K1, P1, K1,* P to end

Row 3: (inc) K1, kfb in next 6 sts, K3, *K1, P1, K1* = *19 sts*

Row 4: as row 2

Row 5: K to last 3 sts; *K1, P1, K1*

Row 6: as row 2

Row 7: (inc) K1, kfb in next 3 sts, K to last 3 sts; *K1, P1, K1* = *22 sts*

Continue in Left Hood Stitch Pattern

Left Hood Stitch Pattern:

Row 1: *K1, P1, K1,* P to end

Row 2: K to last 3 sts; *K1, P1, K1*

These two rows form the pattern stitch

Continue as follows:

Rows: 3 – 33: Repeat rows 1 – 2, **fifteen more times,** then work **row 1** *only,* once more

Cast off all sts in pattern loosely

Continue on to Back

Charter ~ From the Sea Collection

Back:

Wrong side facing, rejoin yarn to **center 26 sts,** work in Back Stitch Pattern

Back Stitch Pattern:

Row 1: P2, K2, (K1, P1) three times, K6, (P1, K1) three times, K2, P2

Row 2: P4, (P1, K1) three times, P6, (K1, P1) three times, P4

These two rows form the pattern stitch
Continue as follows:

Rows 3 – 17: Repeat rows 1 – 2, **seven more times,** then work **row 1 *only*, once more**

Continue on to Shape Shoulders

Shape Shoulders:

Next Row: Cast off 8 sts, K1, P6, (K1, P1) three times, P4

Next Row: Cast off 8 sts, P1, K6, P2

Continue on to Back Hood Panel

Back Hood Panel:

Continue and work as follows:

Next Row: K2, P6, K2

Next Row: (inc) P2, kfb in next 6 sts, P2 = *16 sts*

Next Row: (inc) K1, kfb in next st, P12, kfb in next st, K1 = *18 sts*

Next Row: (inc) P3, K2, kfb in next 8 sts, K2, P3 = *26 sts*

Continue in Back Hood Stitch Pattern

Back Hood Stitch Pattern:

Row 1: (right side) K3, P to last 3 sts; K3

Row 2: P3, K to last 3 sts; P3

These two rows form the stitch pattern

Continue as follows:

Rows 3 – 23: Repeat rows 1 – 2, **ten more times,** then work **row 1 *only*, once more**

Cast off all sts in pattern loosely

Continue on to Right Front

Charter ~ From the Sea Collection

Right Front: (Includes 3 sts worked in seed stitch for button band indicated in *italics*)

Wrong side facing, work on **remaining 17 sts** in Right Front Stitch Pattern

Right Front Stitch Pattern:

Row 1: P2, K1, (P1, K1) 3 times, P5, *K1, P1, K1*

Row 2: *K1, P1, K1,* K5, (P1, K1) three times, P3

These two rows form the pattern stitch

Continue as follows:

Rows 3 – 5: Repeat rows 1 – 2, **one more time,** then work **row 1** *only,* **once more**

Row 6: (4th buttonhole) *K1, YO, K2tog,* K5, (P1, K1) three times, P3

Rows 7 – 16: Repeat rows 1 – 2, **five more times**

Continue on to Shape Shoulder

Shape Shoulder:

Next Row: Cast off 8 sts, P5, *K1, P1, K1*

Next Row: *K1, P1, K1,* K6

Continue on to Right Hood Panel Shaping

Right Hood Panel Shaping: (Includes 3 sts worked in seed stitch for band edging indicated in *italics*)

Wrong side facing, continue as follows:

Row 1: P6, *K1, P1, K1*

Row 2: (inc) *K1, P1, K1,* K1, kfb in next 4 sts, K1 = *13 sts*

Continue . .

Right Hood Panel Shaping Cont

Row 3: P to last 3 sts; *K1, P1, K1*

Row 4: (inc) *K1, P1, K1,* K3, kfb in next 6 sts, K1 = *19 sts*

Row 5: as row 3

Row 6: *K1, P1, K1,* K to end

Row 7: as row 3

Row 8: (inc) *K1, P1, K1,* K12, kfb in next 3 sts, K1 = *22 sts*

Continue in Right Hood Stitch Pattern

Right Hood Stitch Pattern:

Row 1: P to last 3 sts; *K1, P1, K1*

Row 2: *K1, P1, K1,* K to end

These two rows form the pattern stitch
Continue as follows:

Rows 3 – 24: Repeat rows 1 – 2, **eleven more times**

Cast off all sts loosely, continue on to Complete

Complete Hood: Right sides together, join shoulder seams. Sew cast off edges of left hood panel to cast off edges of right hood panel, this will create a seam at the top of hood. Align the center of this top seam to center of cast off edge on back hood panel and sew together, proceed to sew row ends of back hood panel to row ends of each side panel, weave in ends.

Continue on to Sleeves

Charter ~ From the Sea Collection

Sleeveless Version: Skip sleeves and continue on to Complete pg 90

Sleeves: Both alike

Sleeve Tip: refer to pg 68

Begin at cuff edge, **cast on 22 sts,** work in Cuff Stitch Pattern

Cuff Stitch Pattern:

Row 1: K across all sts

Row 2: (wrong side) K across all sts

Row 3: * K1, P1; rep from * to end

Row 4: as row 3

Row 5: as row 1

Row 6: as row 2

These six rows **complete** the cuff

Next Row: (inc) K5, kfb in next 12 sts, K5 = 34 sts

Next Row: (wrong side) K across all sts

Continue on to Sleeve Stitch Pattern

Sleeve Stitch Pattern:

Row 1: K6, (P1, K1) four times, P6, (K1, P1) four times, K6

Row 2: P6, (K1, P1) four times, K6, (P1, K1) four times, P6

These two rows form the pattern stitch
Continue as follows:

Rows 3 – 10: Repeat rows 1 – 2, **four more times**

Rows 11 – 12: K across all sts

Rows 13 – 18: Repeat rows 1 – 2, **three more times**

Rows 19 – 20: K across all sts

Rows 21 – 24: Repeat rows 1 – 2, **two more times**

Continue on to Shape Sleeve Top

Charter ~ From the Sea Collection Cont

Shaping Tip: refer to pg 68

Shape Sleeve Top:

Right side facing, work as follows:

Row 1: Cast off 3 sts, K2, (P1, K1) four times, P6, (K1, P1) four times, K6

Row 2: Cast off 3 sts, P2, (K1, P1) four times, K6, (P1, K1) four times, P3

Row 3: Cast off 3 sts, K1, (P1, K1) three times, P6, (K1, P1) four times, K3

Row 4: Cast off 3 sts, P1, (K1, P1) three times, K6, (P1, K1) three times, P2

Row 5: Cast off 3 sts, (P1, K1) two times, P6, (K1, P1) three times, K1, P1

Row 6: Cast off 3 sts, * K2tog; rep from * to last st; P1 = *9 sts*

Cast off remaining sts

Continue on to Complete

Complete: Right sides together, join sleeve seams to beginning of sleeve top shaping. Wrong side facing, insert to cast off stitches of armhole opening, sew evenly around opening. Sew on buttons.

Completed Measurement: approx. 6 ¾" from cast on edge to shoulder seam, with a sleeve length of approx. 5 ½" from cuff edge to top of sleeve cap.

Eyelet Beret ~ From the Sea Collection

Model wearing **Eyelet Beret** paired with **Adrift**

Pattern Features: The pattern has been written out with line-by-line instructions given along with variations for working contrast color. A versatile beret taken from my Newsboy Cap with an eyelet row offering creativity with various ribbon choices added

Construction: Worked flat: Back and forth in rows, from the brim to crown in one piece then seamed

Materials: 50 – 65 yards (1 – 1 ¼ ounces) of worsted weight yarn

Knitting Needles: Pair of 3.25mm throughout (US 3-UK/CANADIAN 10)

Notions: 1 Button size ½" (12mm) used for decoration on top of crown, Darning Needle, 1 yd of ¼" (7 mm) ribbon for threading through eyelet row if desired

Gauge: Using 3.25mm needles: 6 sts and 7 rows in 1in over stockinette stitch

Skill Level:

BEGINNER   EASY

Main Body:

Begin at lower edge and **cast on 46sts,** work as follows:

(Variation: cast on in contrast and work rows 1 – 2)

Rows 1 – 2: Work in **garter stitch**

(Variation: break contrast, join on main color and continue)

Rows 3 – 4: Beginning with a <u>knit row,</u> work in **stockinette stitch**

Row 5: (inc) K1, * kfb in next st, rep from * to last st; K1 = *90 sts*

Row 6: P across all sts

Row 7: (eyelet row) K1, * YO, K2tog, rep from * to last st; K1

Row 8: P across all sts

Row 9: (inc) * K8, kfb in next 2 sts, rep from * to end = *108 sts*

Rows 10 – 13: Beginning with a <u>purl row,</u> work in **stockinette stitch** (Variation: work row 13 in contrast color)

Continue as follows:

– 91 –

by Debonair Designs ~ copyright © 2011 - 2013 Debonair Designs

Eyelet Beret ~ From the Sea Collection Cont

(Variation: work row 14 in contrast color)

Row 14: (wrong side) K across all sts to form a ridge

(Variation: break contrast and continue in main color)

Rows 15 – 16: Beginning with a **knit row,** work in **stockinette stitch**

Row 17: (dec) * K8, K2tog, K2tog; rep from * to end = *90 sts*

Row 16: P across all sts

Continue on to Crown

Crown:

Row 1: (dec right side) * K8, K2tog; rep from * to end = *81 sts*

Rows 2, 4, 6, 8, 10, 12, 14: P across all sts

Row 3: (dec) * K7, K2tog; rep from * to end = *72 sts*

Row 5: (dec) * K6, K2tog; rep from * to end = *63 sts*

Row 7: (dec) * K5, K2tog; rep from * to end = *54 sts*

Row 9: (dec) * K4, K2tog; rep from * to end = *45 sts*

Row 11: (dec) * K3, K2tog; rep from * to end = *36 sts*

Row 13: (dec) * K2, K2tog; rep from * to end = *27 sts*

Row 15: (dec) * K1, K2tog; rep from * to end = *18 sts*

Row 16: (dec) * P2tog; rep from * to end = *9 sts*

Continue on to Complete

Complete: Break yarn and thread through remaining stitches, drawing up firmly and fasten securely. Join seam, thread ribbon choice through eyelet row starting at desired side, fasten and form a bow or work a twisted cord. **Tip:** refer to pg 68. Sew on button at top of crown. **Completed Measurements:** Designed to fit head circumference of 13" (33cm) approx.

SEASONAL HAND KNITTED DESIGNS FOR 18" DOLLS ~ SPRING/SUMMER COLLECTION

MEET THE MODELS

The models are all by the German Company, Götz ® Learn more about them on following pages.
From the 2003 Precious Day Collection™ meet Julia, Jessica, and Elisabeth
From the 2001 Little Sisters Collection™ meet Tess (rewigged), Tess (original wig), Teyla (Tess rewigged) & Katie

These 18 inch Gotz model dolls all share the same articulated body type as the American Girl Dolls ®

Julia

Jessica

Elisabeth

Tess

Tess

Teyla

Katie

- 93 -

by Debonair Designs ~ copyright © 2011 - 2013 Debonair Designs

SEASONAL HAND KNITTED DESIGNS FOR 18" DOLLS ~ SPRING/SUMMER COLLECTION

ABOUT THE MODEL DOLLS

The models I make use of are from the well-respected German doll manufacturing company known as **Götz**, a German company with an American subsidiary based in Baldwinsville, United States. Marianne and Franz Gotz founded Götz Puppenfabrik in 1950. The first dolls were made of paper maché and were crafted with the help of five family members and sold directly to the public by Franz Götz.

These models were produced as a line of children's play dolls, that share the same soft cloth body type as the popular American Girl Dolls ®, which is not surprising since Götz aided in the assembly of what was known as *'Pleasant Company American Girl dolls'* during the 1990's at their Baldwinsville location. The factory closed in 2004 and the site in Germany closed shortly thereafter. Today these dolls can be mostly found via secondary market sites like eBay.

Shares the same articulated body type as American Girl Dolls Little Sisters Tess shown here with Jess, an American Girl Doll

These play dolls stand 18" with full vinyl arms and legs articulated at the top with ball joints in order to hold a pose.

Read more about the lines that were produced along with pictures for identifying them and learn about their differences.

- 94 -

by Debonair Designs ~ copyright © 2011 - 2013 Debonair Designs

SEASONAL HAND KNITTED DESIGNS FOR 18" DOLLS ~ SPRING/SUMMER COLLECTION

ABOUT THE MODEL DOLLS

The models I make use of are from the well-respected German doll manufacturing company known as Götz.

Götz 'Little Sisters Collection' ~ 2001 – 2002

The *'Little Sisters'* line were produced by Götz, but were sold under, *'Dolls Unlimited'*, a division of idols, in the years 2001 and 2002. The three dolls in this line are: **Lily**, a blue eyed blond with full bangs, **Tess**, a brown eyed brunette also with full bangs and **Katie**, a blue/gray eyed strawberry blond with center part, pictured wearing their starter outfits. The face mold used for this line is known as the *'Mona Lisa'* face mold, they are fully articulated having the ability to hold their position with ball joints in their vinyl arms and legs just like the American girl dolls and were made so they have a slightly pigeon toed stance with beautiful open and close sleep eyes and soft eye lashes. This particular line only have high quality Kanekalon wigs, identifying markings stamped on the back of their neck is mold number 305/16 and their heads are attached to their bodies by string ties such as the American Girl dolls.

Götz used the same *'Mona Lisa'* face mold for a new updated version, called the *'Precious Day Collection'*. The *'Precious Day'* name has been used by Götz for many years, first just for babies, then also for these 18" girl play dolls starting in 2002, this was the year after Götz stopped making the *"Little Sisters Collection'*. The *"Precious Day Collection'* dolls have the exact same body as the *"Little Sisters'*, with the exception of the pigeon toed stance. Although they share the same face mold, the difference between the two lines is found in the hair. Their hair is not Kanekalon, but instead a high quality synthetic hair that is machine rooted into the vinyl head and most often have some kind of bangs to cover the seam produced from the rooted hair.

by Debonair Designs ~ copyright © 2011 - 2013 Debonair Designs

SEASONAL HAND KNITTED DESIGNS FOR 18" DOLLS ~ SPRING/SUMMER COLLECTION

ABOUT THE MODEL DOLLS

The *'Precious Day'* line also included Asian and Latino dolls, Alicia and Kimberly in the first two years, that made use of a different face mold but was later dropped from the collection.

Alicia, an Hispanic doll with a darker complexion and black eyes that came wearing a three piece casual suit and

Kimberly, an oriental doll with dark brown hair and eyes that came wearing a pink jumper paired with a white printed top

Meet the other dolls in the *'Precious Day'* collection

Elisabeth, a brown eyed brunette with layered hair

Julia, a blue/gray eyed red head also with layered hair and

Jessica, a blue eyed layered blond

by Debonair Designs ~ copyright © 2011 - 2013 Debonair Designs

ABOUT THE MODEL DOLLS

Toward the end of 2003, Götz added two more dolls to the collection.

Ashley, a blue eyed brunette who wore pink plaid capris and a light pink tee-shirt.

and **Emily,** a brown eyed blond, who came wearing jeans with a tee-shirt featuring pink hearts and a hot pink nylon jacket. Emily was produced one time only in December of 2003.

These updated versions had two or three piece outfits that were modern in design with all skirts or dresses and each year they changed their outfits with the original outfits having socks, shoes and dresses only.

" *I hope that this guide along with their identification photos have been helpful and knowledgeable, I will be more than happy to help with any further questions, please feel free to contact me via my email address given for pattern support* "

~ *Deb*

Source: Internet Research

Disclaimer: Debonair Designs is not affiliated with any doll or doll clothing companies.

ACKNOWLEDGMENTS

With a thankful heart to my loving husband and mentor Todd, for encouraging my heart's desire; his insightful words of wisdom kept me strong in my convictions; to our children Nathan and Mariah, for also lending their support and assiting my efforts in any way they could.

A huge thank you to my wonderful test knitters and customers for their contribution and support in knitting my patterns, and with my deepest thanks and appreciation to my internet friends/fellow knitters and doll collectors on Ravelry, whose enthusiasm, love and support played an active role and vital contribution to the finalising of these patterns.

~ Deb

"Yesterday is history, tomorrow is a mystery, today is God's gift, that's why we call it the present"

~ Joan Rivers

ABOUT THE AUTHOR/DESIGNER

Deb, designer/author of this publication, also known as Debonair Designs, was born and raised in England, where her mom taught her the art of knitting at a tender young age.

In 1991 she met and married her American husband while on vacation in the US, and has lived there ever since. Her first introduction to the popular American Girl Dolls came in 2006, since she was already knitting sweaters for teddy bears, her husband suggested she knit for these dolls too, and so began her love affair designing and knitting for dolls.

Today she can be found enjoying new territories after relocating to the evergreen state of Washington, in the Pacific Northwest, just across the Sound from Seattle, along with her husband, their two teenaged children and playful kitty cat, Ginger.

> *I have learnt that something positive always grows out of every change as 2010 brought a new area for me and a passion to fulfill, that of putting pen to paper and writing up knitting patterns for 18" dolls, thanks in large part to an awe-inspiring forum called Ravelry, that made this dream a reality. Today, not wanting to stagnate and always passionate to develop and/or improve upon designs, yet keeping an eye on fashion trends, is important to me. Having a loving support system of family and friends encourages my craft to new heights. I hope you have as much fun with this pattern collection as I did creating it.*
>
> ~ Deb

For pattern support, please feel free to contact Deb with your comments and/or questions: Email: debonair@tekayintl.com

OTHER PUBLICATION

SEASONAL HAND KNITTED DESIGNS FOR 18" DOLLS
Fall/Winter Collection

16 hand knitted pattern designs in a five collection volume that is suitable for both the beginner and seasoned knitter, created not only for your doll's seasonal wardrobe, but for you, the knitter, in celebration in the art of knitting, and in honor of my Mom, Brenda, who taught me the art of knitting at a young age. This Fall/Winter Collection has been fashioned to coordinate with each other for complete ensembles, from the versatile options found in the Sienna Collection, along with the trendy jacket set of the Sinclair Collection (cover), to the stylish essentials offered in the Pemberton Collection and the traditional Gansey inspired sweater set of the Archipelago Collection, finishing with timeless classics found in the Christmas Collection, each design is worked with your doll's ease of dressing in mind.

~ Debonair Designs

DESIGNED TO FIT:

American Girl Dolls ®
& the comparable 18" Gotz ® Dolls,
sized for 18" dolls that share the same body type.

26342946R00057

Printed in Great Britain
by Amazon